BACK ON COURSE
Drive Business Performance
Through Golf

Connie Charles
and Dave Bisbee

ISBN-13: 978-1540538291
ISBN-10: 154053829X

Printed in the United States of America

Edited by Diane Sears, DiVerse Media, www.di-verse-media.com

Cover design and layout by Jill Shargaa, Shargaa Illustrations & Design, www.shargaa.com

The publisher offers discounts on this book when ordered in quantity. Please contact iMapGolf at 1-800-815-0185 or info@imapgolf.com. Visit www.iMapGolf.com for additional information on programs and services.

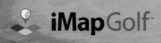

DEDICATION

The two of us certainly interacted with the game in very different ways, and it is that very fact which proves the premise of this book: Business and golf are inexorably linked. The value of relationships the game can create might lead to otherwise unlikely partnerships... like the one between the "golf pro" and the "business pro" resulting in this book.

So we dedicate *Back On Course* to all those business professionals who get it. Who doggedly chase that little white ball down the fairway, out of sand traps, and ultimately into the cup. Who recognize the intrinsic and extrinsic rewards playing this game provides both personally and professionally.

May your golf ball always curve in the direction of the dogleg and your putts always break toward the hole. And may the wind be always at your back.

PLAY ON!

CONTENTS

FOREWORD

I have been in the industry of golf for more than three decades as a PGA Professional and close to 20 years with the PGA Tour. I have overseen the construction of a number of golf clubs and facilities for the PGA Tour, managed a number of world-class country clubs and even owned a golf club along the way.

One important lesson I learned a long time ago stands true to this day: The golf course is the place to build relationships in life and in the world of business. Although the game continues to evolve with technology, agronomy and even the culinary likes and dislikes of the members and guests, one thing that has never changed is the value of spending time with another human being on a golf course.

I have been a witness up close and personal to a few of the largest corporate mergers in American business, all conducted on a golf course. I have also been witness to individuals coming together for the first time on a golf course and forging longstanding relationships that positively change lives. I have seen foundations formed that affect thousands,

platforms created that impact millions, and initiatives launched that change the course of an entire industry, all conducted on a golf course. It truly is the place to build relationships in life and in business.

I'm sure you will find *Back On Course* a great and interesting read. It's also a roadmap for bringing business and golf together in a powerful and meaningful way that is sure to increase bottom-line performance. And best of all, it shows how golf is elevating and fostering the power of relationship-building to another level.

The future of golf and business together has never been more exciting!

Bill Hughes
Master Professional PGA of America
General Manager/Regional Director of Golf
Tournament Players Club Network
PGA TOUR Golf Course Properties

INTRODUCTION: THE BUSINESS OF GOLF

Golf and business, business and golf. They go together like peanut butter and jelly. They've been linked for longer than anyone alive today can remember. Why is that? We've discovered some answers that we're confident will help you with your own career ... and your golf game, too.

We wrote this book as a team, and we've consulted dozens of golfers and business leaders for their insights. We hope you'll enjoy some of their stories we've included throughout the book. First, let's start with our stories.

Thank you for joining us!

Connie Charles and Dave Bisbee

CONNIE'S STORY

I did not grow up golfing. I was one of those girls who got left behind when my father and brother went out to play. Not that I didn't want to play — I was just told it wasn't a game for girls. But I did know I was missing out.

So my entry into the business of golf was purely accidental. I had left my corporate job with DuPont to go out on my own as a consultant. While working at DuPont in training and development for the electronic imaging business, I had been introduced to an assessment tool that captured my imagination, and I knew I wanted to specialize in it.

The Birkman Method was developed by Dr. Roger Birkman in the 1950s. It's unique in that it describes four different layers of a person, whereas most assessments address only one. Because of its complexity, it creates one of the most accurate pictures of an individual available, all gleaned from a questionnaire that takes 30 to 40 minutes to fill out. It describes what you're passionate about, your natural strengths, what you need from others in order to excel, and how your behaviors change when you get under stress.

A colleague and I had created some pretty amazing initiatives using data from The Birkman Method. We had seen people and their organizations achieve new levels of success through better self-awareness and self-management. I knew I had discovered a unique way to help people improve performance both personally and professionally, and I decided that would be my life's mission.

One day I called Birkman International. I was on friendly terms with the person who happened to take my call. He said, "I just got this really weird phone call from a guy who owns a golf school in Scottsdale, Arizona. He thinks there is an application of the data we produce to how people play golf. Do you want to call him and see what it's about?"

That's how it began. Totally serendipitous. Although at that point I had never swung a club, I knew the connection between business and golf was powerful, and this was my opportunity to get inside the ropes.

Over the next couple of years, I spent lots of time on the golf course and even bought my first set of custom clubs. And it turned out the golf school owner was right. Not only did the data we worked with improve business performance in the corporate world, but we could use the same data to improve people's scores on the golf course. The same principles applied to the golf course or the conference room. It was just a lot more fun when the classroom was the golf course.

Today, after 25 years of using The Birkman Method, my team has reached a level of sophistication that allows us to apply the data to almost any situation. For golfers, we have developed a shorter questionnaire that gives us similar accuracy but in a much more focused way. It takes only 10 minutes to complete and still looks at the four layers of an individual's personality. We now have a way to help people understand what keeps them motivated to play, know their strengths and how to use them, manage their environment so they can play their best, and respond to stressors in a way that keeps them in control.

CONNIE CHARLES

In our earlier days of combining golf and The Birkman Method, what we were doing was so revolutionary that in some ways it was ahead of its time. People didn't get it until they experienced it. So we started a marketing campaign to attract key decision-makers to an Executive Golf School. We began with a purchased list and then had a process for qualifying it by calling to find out whether the executives were golfers. Most of the time, if they were, they took our call.

In advance of the event, participants were asked to complete our questionnaire. The day started with a workshop where they learned about their unique approach to the game through their individual golf profiles. The profile results were always spot-on, which was a little spooky for some people. Invariably, someone at some point would raise a hand and say, "This would be fantastic to have at work."

Bingo, we were in! It was an easy segue to talk about their profiles as leaders and how we could help their businesses. And not only did they intellectually understand, but we were able to demonstrate out on the practice range how a better comprehension of who you are could change your performance when you had a club in your hands. Our favorite story was of one person who actually shot a hole in one the next day at a tournament. He gave us some credit, although not a share of the winnings!

So why golf? What's so special about this game that makes it a unique business tool? Business golf is about relationships. Our strategy was to give people something they love in order to earn the right to sell them something they need. In a very short amount of time, you can build a lifetime relationship with someone you previously had never known — especially if you fix that person's slice.

Additionally, golf simulates what goes on in the business environment. The same skills you need to run a great business are required for a great round of golf: adapting to changing conditions, making strategic as well as tactical decisions, managing your tools and resources, and more.

But most of all, it's about people. And that's why my colleague Dave Bisbee and I have written this book. It's time for business to get back on course — the golf course. The quality of relationships will impact the performance of your business, and there is no better place to build great relationships than in a five-hour meeting on the golf course.

But business has lost its way with regard to golf. Although the financial expenditure in business golf is still enormous, many business leaders are looking for ways to better monetize their investment. That's what this book is about: how to use golf as a tool to build relationships that encourage people to want to do business with you.

I met Dave through a series of serendipitous connections. We often joke about how it's like bringing peanut butter and jelly together. Both are great in and of their own, but put them together and you get a new type of magic.

Dave has brought golf credibility to the equation. His expertise in teaching people how to improve their ability to hit a golf ball is unquestioned, and people seek him out just for that purpose. When we were hosting Executive Golf Schools as a way of introducing ourselves to the business community, his ability to fix someone's swing went a long way toward building loyalty among our prospects.

I remember three executives from a financial services company who attended one of our events in Keystone, Colorado. They were so excited about what they learned that the follow-up meetings were easy to schedule. One of the execs brought us in immediately to facilitate a team meeting for his portion of the business. This went so well that they asked their vice president of human resources to work with us to put together a plan for the company.

When the company went through a reorganization that required relocation, the VP of HR made the decision to not move, and he joined our team as one of our executive consultants. And it all started with golf.

DAVE'S STORY

To say that golf has been a big part of my life would be an understatement. I started playing when I was 5 years old with an old cut-down 3-wood the local pro gave me. It was meant to be a distraction so my mother, who was a pretty good amateur golfer, could practice in peace. The distraction turned into an obsession. I started working at the golf course when I was 12, gave up my amateur status when I was 15, and never looked back.

My golf career has taken me to just about every corner of the globe and involved almost every facet of the industry. I tried to play on the professional tours, worked as a club pro at various facilities, designed and built golf clubs for a number of the top manufacturers, and taught the game for some of the most recognized golf schools in the country. It was that last item on the list that captured my attention and became my life's work.

DAVE BISBEE (ON THE RIGHT)

Teaching the game became the focus of my career, and I opened my first golf school in 1989. Back then, technology was in its infancy. Video swing analysis was just starting to be developed that could capture slow-motion images of a golfer's swing. Perimeter-weighted clubs were the latest advancement in golf equipment, and to figure out how far it was to your target you had to count the number of steps it took and then calculate the yardage.

Fast-forward to today, and it's remarkable how technology has had an impact on the game. I now use my cell phone to capture video that I can share in real time with a student. Golf clubs are outfitted with motion-sensing equipment that can detect swing plane, tempo, face position and club speed, and that data can be downloaded to an app on your phone which can provide error detection and prescribe corrections.

I have always tried to stay on the leading edge of these innovations and can only imagine what will hit the market in the next few years. Technology has unquestionably changed the way students and instructors engage in the learning process. However, one of the fundamental elements of the teacher/student interface has been missing: a way to identify what's going on inside the mind of the golfer.

I certainly understood that all of my students brought unique personality traits to the course when they played, and I became a student of the "sports psychology" movement and attempted to integrate some of those themes into my curriculum, but I knew it was little more than fluff. I was looking for something more tangible that could connect the internal game with the external game.

Little did I know that forces at work behind the scenes would lead me to that missing puzzle piece. I will not bore you with the unlikely series of coincidences that led a mutual acquaintance to introduce me to Connie Charles. But the rest, as they say, is history.

When Connie first introduced me to the assessment tool she was using in corporate applications and showed me how it had been adapted to golf, it changed my world. It also began a collaboration that has spanned more than 20 years. The profile became the starting point for my instruction process. The tool took my teaching to a different level because it gave me the ability to understand individual motivations for playing, determine how to relate to someone's unique learning style, and recognize stress behaviors so I could help golfers develop coping strategies.

It didn't take long for some of my students who were executives, and played the game for more than just the recreational aspect, to see how this could relate back at the office. At the same time, Connie was beginning to explore the possibilities of combining something people liked … golf … with something they needed … executive development. We teamed up, and the result was the Executive Golf School that we used to showcase the different business solutions we could provide. To use a mixed metaphor, the concept was a home run.

The experience of conducting Executive Golf Schools inevitably led us to develop a series of golf-centric programs such as the Strategic Scramble, a team-building event conducted on the golf course; Business Golf Essentials, a program designed to teach executives or companies to use the game as a business strategy; and Decision Drivers, a program aimed at improving sales skills. As companies engaged with us through these unique programs, we began to understand the deep connection between the game of golf and corporate culture.

We also became aware of the challenges participating in the game presented. Golf got a pretty bad rap during the economic crisis, and many companies tried to distance themselves from the game to avoid the perception that they were wasting corporate dollars on lavish perks like country club memberships or golf outings. The game had an image problem.

Connie and I believe the game of golf and the business world are inexorably connected. And that's the reason we've written this book. There is no other game or activity that can pay the same kinds of dividends as golf. The setting of the golf course breaks down barriers so you can build relationships, gain insights into personalities, and enjoy a shared experience that keeps you top of mind when a company is looking for a partner in business.

Our goal is to re-establish the vital business/golf connection by clearly illustrating how a company can improve bottom-line results when it leverages the game. The mission to "put business back on course" will challenge the golf industry and the business community to work together to bring the game out of the shadows. We hope our work and this book can be the catalyst.

1

WHY GOLF IS A BIG DEAL

The game of golf has been around for a long time. In fact, there are accounts dating back to the Roman Empire of a game known as Paganica, which was played using a bent stick to hit a leather ball that was stuffed with feathers. It might be a bit of a stretch to give the Romans credit for starting the game we know today, but it does show that the human race seems to have some inherent attraction to hitting a ball with a stick.

How popular is golf? Today the game generates $76 billion in economic impact. That figure is more than the combined value of the National Football League, Major League

> " *The best selling environment in the world is spending four hours in a golf cart with a business prospect.*
>
> — William C. Murphy,
> VP for major account sales,
> Hewlett-Packard "

Baseball, the National Basketball Association, and the National Hockey League. Golf is played in 119 countries on 32,000 courses by 57 million people worldwide. That's right, golf is a big deal.

HOW IT ALL STARTED

The history of the modern game is usually attributed to Scotland in the 15th century. The game got off to a rough start, with the Scottish Parliament banning it because it interfered with archery practice, which was vital to national defense. King James II enforced the ban until 1491. Sometime soon after the ban was lifted, King James IV took up the game, and its popularity and reputation as a pastime of royal indulgence was set.

As time progressed, the game evolved. The Honorable Company of Edinburgh Golfers drafted the first Rules of Golf in 1744. Competitions back then were informal affairs consisting mainly of matches that involved participants betting against each other and with spectators.

This all changed in 1860 with the establishment of the Open Championship, also known as the British Open. The die was cast for what would become the staple of professional tour 72-hole events we enjoy today.

Golf took a while to find traction in the United States. In fact, the first golf course wasn't built until 1888 in Yonkers, New York. The Amateur Golf Association — later to become the U.S. Golf Association — was formed in 1894, and it soon held the first formal National Open Championship. First prize paid $150. My, how times have changed.

Play for pay created the need for another organizing body to differentiate professionals from amateur golfers. In 1916, the Professional Golfers Association (PGA) was formed and a new phase of what would drive the popularity of the game began to take shape.

CELEBRITY STATUS

Professional golfers became celebrities, and the attention the sport was generating began to attract corporate sponsorship of players and events. Arnold Palmer is almost universally recognized as the catalyst that solidified the game's now inseparable bond with the business community. His charisma made television ratings rise, and America's top brands lined up to put their logos on hats, shirts, golf bags, even blimps.

To be associated with the game was almost a requisite if you wanted your company to be recognized as relevant and successful. The corporate connection to the game became so strong that companies like IBM, National Cash Register, DuPont, Firestone and TRW, to name a few, built their own golf courses so employees could enjoy the game and the company could entertain customers. Many of those venerable clubs still exist today.

In 1937, Bing Crosby, an avid golfer with a 2 handicap, had an idea to start a golf tournament. The goal was to bring together his Hollywood friends who loved to play, some golf professionals who might like to hang out with celebrities, and some wealthy individuals who might have an interest in investing in Hollywood projects. These groups would play in a team event that culminated in a clambake for the participants.

Sam Snead won the first tournament and received a check for $500. In 2015, Brandt Snedeker won the event, now known as the AT&T Pebble Beach National Pro-Am, and took home a check for more than $1.2 million.

A BOOMING INDUSTRY

The PGA Tour's estimated payout for 2015 was more than $350 million in prize money. The association set new records in charitable contributions in 2014 by donating more than $140 million. No other professional sports organization even comes close.

In addition to those involved in the Tour, there's another group of people serving on the true front lines of the initiative to put business back on course: PGA Professionals. They are the ambassadors of the game to the recreational golfer. They promote the game to beginners, teach the game, sell the equipment and run the tournaments.

For the savvy business golfer, PGA Professionals can be valuable strategic partners. You should think of the golf course as an extension of your office, and your local PGA Professional as almost your vice president of sales.

How do you join the legions of people who are combining their love of the game with their ambition to become the best in business? By understanding how to leverage this very powerful tool. And by the same method legendary comedian Jack Benny joked around was the way to get to Carnegie Hall in New York: Practice, practice, practice.

ECONOMIC IMPACT IN THE U.S.

o $28 billion in revenue earned at golf facilities

o $6.1 billion in purchases of golf clubs, balls and apparel

o $5.6 billion in tournaments, endorsements and charities

o $3.6 billion in golf course capital investment

o $18 billion in hospitality and tourism

o $15 billion in real estate investments

GOLF GENERATES
$76.3 BILLION
IN ECONOMIC
IMPACT ANNUALLY

GOLF AROUND THE WORLD

o In business, influences up to $30 billion in sales

o Played in 119 countries

o Played on 32,000 courses

o Played by 57 million worldwide

o Played in 800,000 rounds annually

ON COURSE WITH ... IAN HUDSON
PRESIDENT, DUPONT EUROPE

Why I play golf: For many reasons: five hours of peace, away from the smart phone, exercising outside, playing the most frustrating game I have ever encountered. The risk/reward equation and resulting disaster or personal satisfaction are present in every shot. Competing against others in match play, and against myself most of the time, is a key attraction of the game also. And being able to spend five hours in the company of my wife at weekends ... even if her handicap is currently lower than mine!

How golf has helped me in business: Having spent 18 months negotiating a contract with an Asian partner, we celebrated the conclusion with a golf match. My own partner played twice a year so was little help. We were three down after nine holes. Not wishing to end on a low point, I changed gears and won on the last hole with an approach to 2 feet! Having "won" the negotiation, I was certainly not going to lose the golf match!

How golf has made me more self-aware: Some days your golf game just comes together and other days it doesn't ... just like in life ... and you really don't know why. As a Type A person, remaining calm and patient is a constant struggle, and golf teaches me every round that I have to keep my emotions in check. Golf is a largely self-policing "rules-based system." If more people played golf and adopted this approach in their personal and professional lives, we would live in a more ethical, corruption-free world.

How golf has helped me develop business relationships: In business encounters, the moment you know that your interlocutor is a golfer, it opens up a whole field of shared experiences, creating immediate common ground. In one business relationship, we were never able to uncover the business opportunity, but we tried really hard on several great golf courses.

Words of wisdom: The best advice for someone taking up golf is to find a pro and take lessons before you ever set foot on the course. Be prepared for the frustrations, and the rewards will come. Golf courses are usually located in nice locations, so combine golf with tourism. The best advice I ever received: You have to decide whether you want to continue being a hacker or become a golfer. If the latter, be prepared for the pain and frustration, but it will be worth it ... and it is.

2

THE UNDENIABLE LINK: GOLF AND BUSINESS

Back in the days when deals were made over three-martini lunches in private booths at the back of a bar, golf developed a reputation as a place for private business conversations. Men played rounds at exclusive country clubs, giving the sport an image as an elitist pastime for people who were wealthy and influential. Women golfers were hobbyists and not taken too seriously.

It was assumed that once men got to the C-suite level, maybe as chief executive officer or chief financial officer, they were going to play golf as part of their work. They had corporate memberships at the best golf courses, and some corporations even had their own courses.

When the Great Recession hit in the late 2000s, golf got thrown into the category of frivolous spending and excess. Gradually many corporations and their executives drifted away from the golf course as a place to do business. It was now considered off-limits, and those deals stopped happening.

Being in the business and knowing the kinds of people we know, we are keenly aware that golf didn't go away as a business tool. It went into the shadows. Many organizations gave up their corporate memberships, but their executives were hooked. They still considered the golf course a place of refuge where they could spend quality time with peers to develop strategic partnerships, look at creating mergers and acquisitions, and brainstorm about big ideas. Women were incorporating golf into their business practices more and more, too, as they rose among the corporate ranks. Golf was truly linked in before LinkedIn. Golf was the way people at the executive level found other opportunities. It became a private networking environment.

Business golf didn't go away — it just became the electrified third rail. Executives understood that society might frown on people who played golf during the business day in a major economic recession, but they continued to play. They were just more discreet about it.

And some organizations hung in there as well. In the depths of the financial crisis, they continued their corporate sponsorship of professional and amateur golf events. They recognized that being aligned with a sport based on integrity, sportsmanship and playing by the rules was good business, especially during a time when distrust surrounded so much of Wall Street.

WHY GOLF MAKES BUSINESS SENSE

There are many reasons corporations want to be associated with golf, but there's one that tops the list: It's good for their brands. When you look at individual golf tournaments, you see the title sponsor with branding all over the advertising, marketing, signage and apparel. Even sub-sponsors get major visibility for participating in ways such as operating corporate hospitality tents.

All of these companies are trying to reach the same audience or portions of the audience. In this way, they can justify to shareholders and customers that it makes good sense to be where they can be visible to buyers who can ensure they make a profit.

Look at the television commercials that air during a tournament. You see logos for products including luxury cars, fashion brands, jewelry, high-end food and beverage, wealth management services, prescription medicine that improves lifestyle. These brands understand how the demographic of the TV spectator aligns with their customer profile.

Golf also offers a good opportunity for multiple impressions, which allows potential customers to view a commercial many times during the same broadcast. If you're buying advertising on a sitcom at night, the show airs for half an hour. A football game airs for three hours, but some people switch channels at halftime. A golf telecast, on the other hand, airs continuously for three hours or more. And even when commercials aren't on the screen, there is a lot of advertising taking place. Tour players wear branding on their apparel and equipment. You see corporate logos on shirts, hats, shoes, golf bags, clubs.

There's another reason golf is a good sport as a branding partner for businesses. You rarely hear about golfers getting into trouble in their private lives. There isn't a parade to the police station as there is in other sports. As a rule, golfers tend to be more mindful of how they conduct themselves in public and private settings. The game is all about etiquette, sportsmanship, self-policing and ethics. Anytime you see a player call a penalty on himself or herself that no one else would have seen, it hits the news cycle because it's unusual in the sports world. Corporations like to align themselves with these values.

HOW GOLF IMITATES THE CORPORATE ENVIRONMENT

In business, you have to take calculated risks to move your organization to the next level. You launch new products, open additional locations, hire more people, change your prices, try different branding strategies. Golfing gives people the same kinds of opportunities. During the course of a round, you're always asking yourself, "Do I go for it or not?" You stretch yourself, make decisions and live with the consequences.

Jordan Spieth takes a shot and it goes into the air and comes up short. Now he has to decide how this will affect the rest of his play on this hole, and how that will impact the rest of the round, and how his performance in this tournament will affect his professional standings. This is a metaphor for business strategy. You have the right club and skillset, but something outside your control intervenes. The decisions you make will affect the future of your organization. This resonates with the business world. Defining moments, known as "Tin Cup moments" after the movie starring Kevin Costner, come along all the time. Either you define the moment or you let the moment define you.

Golf imitates business in many other ways:

The team aspect. Today on the pro golf tour you hear more players talking about the team. An individual is standing there with club in hand, accepting accolades or criticism. But there is always a team involved, and the decisions you make and the way you perform affect the team.

The caddy-player relationship. Most players don't go out and walk the golf course to mark yardages and take the topography of the green. They rely on the caddy to do that research and get the lay of the land, understand how far it is from Point A to Point B, and read whether the player is on his game or not. The caddy is involved in the decision- making on the right club to use for the shot. The caddy is second in command. Caddies don't hit the shots, but they have influence on what is going on. The player influences how much money the caddy earns and how his job goes. The caddy's success depends on the success of the player.

Sponsor performance. The sponsor puts money on the player, and if that golfer misses the cut, the sponsor loses the opportunity for the player to be seen — which is like paying for a billboard that is never installed. Sponsors are like an organization's strategic partners. Every player represents an organization. The player is the leader, and that individual's actions can affect even entities outside of the immediate circle.

Teamwork. There is hardly any better metaphor for what happens in the business world than an alternate-shot tournament like the Ryder Cup. One player tees off and another player hits from where that shot falls. The team members alternate shots. Everything one player does has a direct effect on the performance of the other person. There are times when you can be knocked out as a team because one person made a mistake. It can challenge your ability to cope with adversity. You either become supportive and help the person deal with the mistake or you become blaming and isolate yourself from the other person. And again, what you do will determine how the organization moves forward.

If you listen to Jordan Spieth when he is talking to the media, he talks about the team as if he's leading an organization of people. Swing coach, family members, caddy, sponsors, all are tied to his brand and his performance. He really gets it.

GOLF SHOWCASES INDIVIDUAL PERSONALITY

Golf as a sport is a great indicator of individual performance in the workplace. We've been teaching about this for many years. Dave describes it this way:

In my experience as a teacher and a coach, I've watched people struggle between the practice tee and the golf course. They leave the practice tee full of hope and optimism and then at the first tee everything falls apart. Something happened from the time they left that practice tee, and they forgot everything and became incapable of reproducing the same results.

You develop your skills on the practice tee, where the shot doesn't count and you don't have to chase the ball. Practice tees are level and don't present the challenging conditions you encounter on the golf course. All of a sudden you're faced with a shot you haven't attempted on the practice tee. The real game is full of those challenges.

I tell students once you've gone through and hit some shots that are warm-ups, go to the place on the driving range where you can hit in less-than-perfect conditions. Throw a ball off to the side in the rough and hit from there. Hit one shot with your driver. Try to imagine what the next shot would be, and hit with that next club. Hit a drive, fairway shot, pitch. Get into a rhythm of playing instead of a rhythm of practice.

Things happen in golf. You get a bad bounce, your ball ends up in the rough, you have to make a specialty shot to get back into play. That happens in business, too. Developing your business skills in a classroom is great, but if things end up where you didn't intend them to go, you have to adjust your strategy and get yourself back into play so you can regain control.

Watching the U.S. Tour, we see it all the time with changes in weather. The morning golfers go out and have a great round, and then a storm rolls in and the afternoon wave has a challenging round. You have to be able to adjust and know when to change your strategy.

In this way, golf can also be an effective tool for checking out a job candidate. When I've tried to hire someone as a golf professional or part of an organization's operational team, playing a round of golf with that individual is ultimately revealing.

There are some clues you can glean from your typical HR process of looking at a resume and conducting an interview, but you're never really seeing the authentic person. You're seeing a portrayal based on what the person wants you to see. The golf course strips that away. If you're looking for someone who's going to come into your organization as an influencer or fit your company culture, the golf course is a great way to compare behaviors in that environment with the results of the interview. Golf reveals the authentic person.

Watch how the individual acts and reacts in a golf setting. When I'm out playing for this specific reason, I'm watching everything from when people show up — early, on time, late — to whether they are prepared. What does it look like when they go through their process of arrival? Do they warm up or go right to the first tee?

I take a look at their golf bag. Checking out their equipment is not about getting an idea of how much money they make, but how they spend money and what is important to them. How are things organized in there? If I'm looking for someone who is going to be involved in finance and accounting, or will work as a CFO, a disorganized golf bag might give me pause. It's like reading the tea leaves.

I watch how they act and react, what kinds of rules they play by, how they react when something goes wrong. I look at what they do when something goes wrong for someone else in the group. Do they help another player find a ball in the weeds? That can indicate how this individual will perform when a co-worker is struggling. Golf strips away the pretense and reveals the authentic person.

These clues carry all the way to the end, through the 19th hole, and when they get into their cars and drive away. How did they handle themselves after the round? At the 19th hole, you're still "on the clock" even though you're going to have a casual beer and share some food. How did this individual debrief and finish things off? There's not another environment that allows you to observe those behaviors before you get the person into the workplace.

ON COURSE WITH ... ROMAINE SEGUIN
PRESIDENT, AMERICAS REGION, UPS INTERNATIONAL INC.

Why I play golf: I enjoy playing golf because it provides me a relaxing environment where I get to combine my two passions of doing exercise and conducting business. I started playing golf 32 years ago when I began my career at UPS. At first, I participated in the sport as a way of supporting charity events, but more and more I found that it's a great avenue to get to know customers. I can't think of a better way of enhancing relationships with people than spending nine or 18 holes of quality time with them.

How golf has helped me in business: A few years ago, when I was working in Minnesota, there was a customer I wanted to do business with, but he was too busy and he was not really interested in talking to me. I found out he enjoyed playing golf, so I used this information as my approach to get my foot in the door. I asked him to come out and play golf with me, and I even offered that if he did, I could get our then-CEO Mike Eskew to someday play with us. That piqued his interest and he took me up on my invitation. We had casual yet compelling conversations that allowed a mutually beneficial business relationship to develop. Unfortunately, Mike and the customer's schedules didn't allow them to get to play golf together, but Mike did visit the customer. That high-level meeting was indirectly possible because of the game.

How golf has made me more self-aware: The sport has taught me the true virtue of patience. I've learned that you have to keep your eye on the prize, remain calm and maintain a positive attitude. Golf is similar to

> "
> *Golf is similar to business, where you can win big or miss your target altogether, but there is always that one shot that will bring you back to the course.*
>
> — Romaine Seguin,
> President, Americas Region,
> UPS International Inc.
> "

business, where you can win big or miss your target altogether, but there is always that one shot that will bring you back to the course. There are good days and there are bad days, but there's always something to make you feel proud of your efforts and allow you to leave the course (and office) feeling accomplished.

How golf has helped me develop business relationships: Building relationships takes time — and just like with golf, which sometimes is a waiting game, you have to be able to put in the hours to come out winning. Through the sport, you have the opportunity to share strategies, tips and, if you're lucky, stories. These stories can open the gates of communication that can lead to the start of fostering personal and business relationships. This pays off even more when you're on a team and you can share your wins and losses together. It's times like these when love for the game can bring dividends that extend off the greens and into the boardroom.

Advice for people thinking of taking up golf: In golf, as in business, you need to be prepared. On the greens it means knowing the etiquette of the sport and who the key players are so you can assess your approach to the game. It doesn't matter if you're not the best player, but knowing the etiquette will help you improve your game and also gain your colleagues' respect. This principle applies to business, too. You need to be prepared before visiting a prospect or showing up for a meeting.

3

POWER TOOLS
FOR SUCCESS

There is one common denominator among most human beings, and that is the desire to succeed. Now, granted, there are a few folks out there who are missing that gene. But for the most part, we all crave the sense of satisfaction that comes from positive achievement. This could be anything from raising a child who thrives to finding the perfect parking space at the mall to building a business empire. The drive for success is a fundamental part of our human nature.

When you sit back and analyze this, it's amazing how the desire to succeed infiltrates so many layers of our lives. Here's an example from Connie:

I was headed through the security line at an airport one day and there was a family ahead of me, obviously decked out for a vacation somewhere warm. The line split and you could go left or right to one of two screening portals. Wife and children went left, hubby turned right. You would have thought there was money on which line was shorter, given the very public display of irritation at hubby for going to the "longer" line.

I went left just because I wanted to follow the drama. The wife's final comment, in as snarky a tone as she could drum up, was, "I'm going to beat you through that screening, so I'll see you on the other side." Hubby relented and joined his wife in the left line, which was disappointing because I was primed to watch the race unfold. However, after I collected my things off the screening belt, my last view of this happy family was of the wife and children standing with arms folded watching hubby, pockets turned inside out, shirt untucked, two TSA agents waving electronic wands past him and saying, "Are you sure you don't have any metal on you?"

Now, that was a silly little story, but it illustrates how we consciously and subconsciously set standards for ourselves to measure our performance. It feels good and rewards our inner self when we achieve them, even if it's something trivial like making it through a security line first.

There are lots of thought leaders out there who have come up with models or theories on how we can do a better job of achieving success. Often this success is linked with the incredibly nebulous concept of happiness. Success is a lot easier to measure, but happiness? That's a more difficult concept to quantify. Still, many of us have spent money in the hopes of discovering how we can achieve success and happiness if we only follow these easy steps.

While there is a lot of goodness embedded in the wide variety of self-help knowledge, why is it that often the theories, methods, processes or three easy steps don't work? It's simple: You're trying to fit into the model rather than fitting the model to you.

Several years back, a software company gave us the ability to compare our golf swing to the swing of a pro. The concept was that if we could only swing like Tiger Woods, we could have the same success. So people went the route of trying to imitate what worked for someone else and expected similar results. Lots of disappointment! The fundamental flaw in this approach is that it makes the assumption that what worked for Tiger would work for you.

That doesn't work. Success comes from a deep understanding of who you are as a person. When you have this knowledge, you can then create a method, a process or a collection of easy steps tailored to you.

The starting point for any success is knowing what you want. That sounds pretty simple, but it can be incredibly difficult to achieve. Sometimes other people shape that definition for us: Your parents tell you to pursue a particular career path, or a boss gives you the metrics for evaluating your business performance. But what you want is really up to you.

In our work with executives, when we sit down with them for the first time to talk about a project, we ask what seems like a pretty simple question: "What do you want out of this initiative?" On occasion, the executive answers with a pretty articulate, well-thought-out response. But it's not unusual to hear, "That's a good question, and I'm not sure."

So at this point you may be wondering, "I thought this was a book about golf and business. Where is this going, anyway?"

While a lot of us focus on the equipment we need in our golf bag to play a great round, there are other "clubs" we need to be able to perform at our best. We refer to these as clubs because just as you would find it difficult to par a hole without a putter, these tools are equally essential when you're playing for business reasons. What can take you from simply a good round of golf to the higher purpose of establishing a business relationship? There are three core drivers:

- Self-awareness
- Self-management
- Relationship management

CLUB 1: SELF-AWARENESS

Our definition of success gives us context. What do you want? When we know what we want, we can then begin the journey of figuring out the best way to get it. If you don't know what you want, you become vulnerable to other people's desires, which may or may not bring you the personal satisfaction and happiness you're seeking.

The ability to figure out what you want begins with a fundamental understanding of who you are. Every thought leader who has developed a model for success agrees with us on this point. The ability to succeed and sustain success is grounded by our self-understanding. So it doesn't matter whether we're working with you as a golfer to help you win the club championship or as a business executive to help you reach this quarter's financial targets, the starting point is the same: you.

The process of self-awareness has three layers or dimensions to it that work together to ensure success:

Layer 1: Your Socialized Behavior
First, your self-awareness has to be an accurate picture of how you come across when you're engaging with other people. This is what we think of as socialized behaviors or how you've learned to be successful through your education, family system and life experiences. It would also include how other people might describe you based on how they experience you.

Layer 2: The Authentic You
This accurate understanding of the "you" on the outside is only the starting point. It must be accompanied by an authentic understanding of the "you"

on the inside. And, sometimes the internal and external views of you can be very different. Here's an example:

Let's take people who are the life of the party and are always invited to be in golf foursomes because their presence guarantees everyone's going to have a great time. They're sociable, they're outgoing and they connect easily even with people they've just met. In fact, no one is a stranger to them. But once you get to know some of these people, you find out they really enjoy getting out on the course by themselves. They covet alone time, space and privacy. Even though they are very good with people, they're introverted. In a case like this, the person on the outside and the person on the inside are very different, yet equally true.

To really understand ourselves and other people, we need to couple an accurate view of our socialized self with an authentic view of who we are on the inside. That's self-awareness.

Layer 3: Your Ability to Describe Yourself
The third layer involves articulating this self-awareness. When we can describe who we are with accuracy and authenticity, then we can begin to shape our world in a way that suits us most. If we don't have this ability to articulate our self-awareness, we set ourselves up for frustration because we're unable to do anything with our self-understanding.

CLUB 2: SELF-MANAGEMENT

Now that we are grounded with an accurate, authentic understanding of ourselves that we can articulate, we're prepared to accelerate the journey to success. It's usually at this point in the process that people start to get a little worried. "What if I'm a failure?" or "Am I OK as is? Do I have what it takes to succeed?" The answer is that you are absolutely perfect. It's true. There is nothing fundamentally wrong with who you are. Where we all run into trouble is that sometimes we don't live in a world that is perfect for us. Does that mean we're doomed to failure? Absolutely not.

Self-management enables us to take that accurate and authentic picture of ourselves and then choose how we want to manage any given situation, even if it's out of our comfort zone. This is not about changing the fundamental picture of who you are. It is instead giving you the power of choice.

When the conditions change on the course, the foursome in front of us slows to a snail's pace, our guest is out of control, or we've just bogeyed another hole, we can choose how we want to respond rather than react. With your self-awareness intact, you can stay in control of your emotions and actions rather than simply reacting to the stress of the situation. We can anticipate how we may respond to any given situation and decide the best way to handle that unique set of circumstances.

Now here's the critical part. The only motivation for managing ourselves differently is when we link the new behaviors to our ability to succeed. That's why knowing what we want is so important. If we're clear on what we want, such as "I want to do business with this person," then we can become intensely motivated to choose the right thoughts, emotions and actions that will take us to that goal.

Think about it. There are so many opportunities for public embarrassment, out-of-control bursts of frustration and expressions of impatience — all things that could make you look like someone no one would want to do business with.

This ability to manage your emotions and actions is the key to successful business golf. If you don't acquire this ability, you increase your risk of not getting what you want because you are no longer making choices.

What should you do differently to ensure you succeed? It's not about changing anything about the perfect you. It's about giving the perfect you the tools to manage yourself so you can take action in the best way that will ensure success.

CLUB 3: RELATIONSHIP MANAGEMENT

It's clear that golf is a great way to build relationships with clients and prospects. Even people who don't play golf accept this as fact. But few people really know how to do it. True, there is a lot of good that happens just through spending time with a person in the same space. Shared experience does indirectly build a bond between you and someone else, especially if there are pictures that document it.

There is more to mine if you know what to look for. Managing relationships is not just an art, it's a science. Each of us is motivated by two things: what we want and what we need. Often we focus exclusively on the want part because that's the easiest to connect with people about. We talk about what we love, and our passions are easy to discuss.

When it comes to the golf course, people could be playing for very different motivations. Some play because they love the scenery. It's all about the total experience: a great day, gorgeous course, beautiful wildlife. Others play to shoot a lower score. They want to reduce their handicap, hit the longest drive, or win the club championship. It's all about measurable progress.

Some people are motivated to play because they love the social aspects of the game. They always play with other people and often love the game within the game: competing for bragging rights or betting on certain aspects of play. They also may love to coach, teach or host events — all aspects that put them in contact with other people.

There's another category of people who play because they love the complexity of the game. They relish the discipline it takes to improve. These folks get serious about their practice and evaluate every single detail that might be linked to performance improvement. Data about their own performance is of vital importance to them.

Once we know what people love about playing golf, then it's easy to build a connection based on a shared sense of what's important in order to enjoy the game. This can be enough, and sometimes it is. But to take your relationship-building with your clients or prospects to the next level, it's important to recognize what they need. This defines the second dimension of motivation. Often it's not obvious to other people because it can be something almost counterintuitive if it's very different from what they love.

Here's an example: There's a person who loves the social aspects of playing golf. He doesn't hesitate to say yes anytime he's invited to play in a charity event. He has even sponsored these events to a pretty sizable amount. He plays often with the same group of guys, and they are always back and forth with who has won the most from each other. However, he doesn't hang around for the dinner afterward, and he's rarely seen at the 19th hole. There was one tournament when he didn't show up at all, even though he was a major sponsor. What gives?

If you had the chance to really get to know this guy, you'd find out that he's a very private person. He craves time alone or with one or two of his closest friends. Even though he comes across like he's the life of the party, he'd really rather not be there in the limelight. What we're seeing here is a contradiction between what someone loves and what that person needs. If we learn to appeal to both, we now have the power of our third club, relationship management.

Now, instead of expecting him to be part of the social scene, we set up private events with him and people he values. He has responded better to an invitation to play a round at a private club than to host that charity event. And if he does sign up, we create "escape routes" so he can exit when he's had enough.

So how do you learn to recognize the hidden needs of a person so you can manage the relationship to a new level? There are two ways.

First of all, we created a questionnaire that simplifies this process. It's called iMapMyGolf and can be accessed at *www.iMapGolf.com.* This 10-minute questionnaire captures four layers of people: what they love, their strengths, what they need, and how they react under stressful circumstances. These reports take the guesswork out of relationship management.

However, if you don't have the benefit of an iMapMyGolf report, there's still another way to figure this out. The key to success with relationships is recognizing that stress behavior is the window to the unmet need. Stress behaviors are reactions to things that don't suit us. When you become skilled at reading these signals, you have the decoder ring to that relationship.

So if your business contact is getting edgy and restless, it shows she needs to get moving. If the behaviors you notice are that your client seems to be getting embarrassed by poor shots and is spending more time off by himself, he needs to have the pressure taken off. Play "best ball" for a couple of holes, letting each player in the foursome hit from the ball that lands in the best position, no matter whose shot got it there.

If your prospect is obsessing about the wind speed, yardage or rules, feed him lots of data and information. Keep things as consistent as possible and don't break the routine. Or if your customer is taking unnecessary risks or making up new rules for play, the round has become boring and you need to lighten things up. Start having some fun rather than just playing the hole.

We see examples of these natural "tendencies" played out every day at the course. A group shows up to play, and inevitably someone insists on being the driver. Another player keeps the scorecard. Another has the role of social director. You can see why we say the golf course is a microcosm of the office. People naturally gravitate to their comfort zones.

While some of this may seem complicated, the reason it works is because people are complex. When integrated into your game, the three corporate power tools of self-awareness, self-management and relationship management will help you turn an average round of golf into a business opportunity.

ON COURSE WITH ... DAVID LARUE
OWNER, BALDWIN SUPPLY COMPANY

The golf course has been a great place for me to build and grow relationships both personally and professionally. The basis of all the warm memories I have for the game started with the ones I treasure so much of going up to Ruttger's Bay Lodge in Northern Minnesota with my family and playing with my father-in-law, Bob Nyrop. Those mornings and afternoons, I learned integrity, patience and proper etiquette. I learned about being a businessman, a father, a golfer and a man.

For the past 15 years, we've hosted a golf tournament for my main business, Baldwin Supply Company in Minneapolis. It's been a special day for our employees, vendors and customers. People look forward to it every year. I usually will play Hole 10 with everyone in the tournament. It's a great chance to connect with our customers and have a bit of competition thrown in there, which makes it fun for everyone. We share a lot of laughs and create great memories.

I love the camaraderie of golf. There is nothing better than having a cigar with some buddies at a beautiful course somewhere in the world. For those few hours, all the stresses of the outside world go away. At the same time, there's something clarifying and minimalistic about the game itself that allows you a deeply private moment of reflection every time you address the ball.

In between the jokes and reminiscences, you have moments of intense awareness of the environment, the lay of the land, the wind. When you step up to the tee, all that matters is what you can do with that little white ball.

Gay Hendricks articulates this best in his book *The Big Leap: Conquer Your Hidden Fear and Take Life to the Next Level* when he says, "The little ball just sits there until you make it go somewhere else. In that regard, golf is very much like life itself: It awaits your intention and action before revealing the mysteries of the outcome."

The ability to blend the intensely personal and the social is one of the most unique and special aspects of the game, and it's exactly like in business. You're trying to outperform yourself, to beat your personal best and improve your results with the ball. Everyone you're there with is doing the same thing. Competition becomes strangely abstract and philosophical here. Sometimes you talk about it, sometimes you don't. Sometimes you think about it, sometimes you don't.

At the end of the day, though, the scorecard is a vast oversimplification of whether or not you performed well. There's so much more going on than you can quantify. And because there's so much going on, so many aspects and facets that can catch the light in so many unique combinations, success on the golf course is a lot like success in business and in life.

The games I've played where I learned from mistakes, the courses that were so beautiful that I can't even remember how the playing went, the games I played where business relationships became friendships, and others where friendships deepened into something truly special ... these were the best games of golf I've played.

In this way, golf has been a great model for me as someone who coaches and mentors people in their lives and careers. Golf has taught me how to define success in meaningful ways, to separate achievement from external rewards in a way I don't think anything else could. Learning this lesson has been crucial to so many of my successes in life and in business.

It's funny to think about just how important playing golf has been. It's funny that it's taken writing about it to say so. As a coach, I'm a big believer in telling the stories of your life because so often it isn't until you sit down to tell your story that the significance of things becomes clear.

Now that I know how important golf has been for me, I wonder how it will change how I play it. I feel a whole new sense of gratitude, a new depth of nostalgia for those games played long ago. I'm going to call and set up a tee time.

> *The little white ball just sits there until you make it go somewhere else. In that regard, golf is very much like life itself: It awaits your intention and action before revealing the mysteries of the outcome.*
>
> — Gay Hendricks,
> author of *The Big Leap: Conquer Your Hidden Fear and Take Life to the Next Level*

4

YOUR SECRET WEAPON: WHAT GOLF CAN REVEAL

Everyone knows great relationships make for great business opportunities. And we all would love to be adept at building those relationships. Some are naturals at it. You've met them. They can walk into any clubhouse and instantly connect. They make friends with people in elevators — and the more floors, the more friends. If you're one of those people, then this chapter will puzzle you. Why do we need to analyze how to build relationships? It comes naturally to you. But not to everyone.

For those who find it more challenging to "meet and greet" and build solid relationships with people who start off as strangers, this chapter will give you some skills to make it easier. And if connecting with people does come easily to you, then what we cover here may help you understand why you're so effective.

Think about a time when you met someone and instantly connected. You may not be able to explain what was happening, but you knew you instantly liked this person. You just knew this person was someone you wanted to be around.

What was going on in that encounter? That person you liked so much was naturally responding to you in a way that matched your interpersonal wiring. The two of you somehow connected, and it was effortless. We're going to discuss how to make those connections intentionally instead of accidentally.

The starting point is understanding that our personalities are actually made up of four different dimensions. We're used to thinking in much more simplistic terms, such as "He's an outgoing person" or "She's an introvert." But actually people are more complex than that, and someone can be both quiet and outgoing. The difference is which aspect of a person would cause him or her to be an introvert in one situation and an outgoing, life-of-the-party type in another.

We've used an assessment tool called The Birkman Method that was developed by Dr. Roger Birkman in the 1950s and describes four different layers of a person: what you're passionate about, your natural strengths, what you need from others in order to excel, and how your behaviors change when you get under stress. After more than 25 years of using this process, we've developed a way to apply it to golfers. The same principles that apply in the workplace also hold true on the greens.

MOTIVATION

The first layer we look at has to do with motivation. It defines why you do what you do and what makes you the happiest. The starting point is what you love to do or what you're passionate about. When you think about why people play golf, generally it's linked to this aspect of their personality. We touched on this earlier in the book. Some people play because they love being outside on a beautiful day enjoying the scenery on a golf course. Others play because they love to be around other people and it's a social experience for them. They would never consider playing by themselves. Some golfers are out there to win the trophy or the club championship, or simply to beat anyone they play. They love competition.

Your first opportunity to connect with someone is based on this dimension, and it's usually pretty easy to figure out if you pay attention. But forcing people to play for the wrong reason is a surefire way to send them home with an unhappy experience. If you have a client who wants to wager or is always asking about the scores of others, the last thing you want to do is suggest that you're out there just to have some fun. If your hot prospect is someone who's more into the Zen of the moment and it's a rainy day, reschedule. If you're playing with Mr. or Ms. Socialite, make sure you have others in your outing who aren't so serious about the game that they take all the fun out of it.

Knowing why people play is the starting point for connecting with someone. When you understand this layer of motivation, you can craft an experience that is something your customer will connect with and want to experience more.

SOCIALIZED BEHAVIOR

The second dimension we look at is also obvious to other people because it represents the person you show to the world. Through your life experiences, your family interaction, your education and mentors along the way, you've learned some behaviors you use to achieve success at whatever you pursue. You may have learned to be decisive or action-oriented, while others may have developed the ability to be thoughtful and reflect on things before they take action.

This socialized behavior is your source of strength because you've gotten very good at it. When the situation calls for your strengths, success is effortless. Think about a time when you were playing at your best. Chances are your strength characteristics absolutely suited the opportunity. Did you move fast and play 18 holes in less than three hours, or did you find yourself completely relaxed and experiencing a balanced sense of rhythm? Were you playing in a competitive tournament with lots of people you liked? Or was your best round when you were totally in control and able to play with a consistency from hole to hole that allowed your best game to come out?

INNER NEED

The next layer isn't so easy to grasp. In fact, it's often hidden to other people and may be surprising even to those who know them well. This is the critical aspect of people that will determine whether or not you're successful in connecting with them and sustaining this relationship over time.

We're talking about what people need from the world around them. We have all developed a set of behaviors that we use to succeed, but sometimes what we need back from the world around us can be very different. In fact, for most people it's an absolutely true statement that the person on the outside is different from the person on the inside. It's no wonder relationships are so challenging, because what you see is not what you get.

Here's an example: Let's say John is always the life of the party. When he shows up to play, everyone has a good time. He is great at meeting and greeting, and he makes everyone in the clubhouse feel comfortable and welcome. No one is a stranger to John — there are just people he hasn't had time to meet yet. However, sometimes after a tournament is over, John is nowhere to be found. In fact, you may get a glimpse of him headed to the parking lot with his golf bag over his shoulder. People are asking, "Where's John?" but either no one knows or there's some excuse like, "He had a phone call to make."

The answer is that even though John has gotten very good at building relationships with people, the "inner" John craves time alone, away from the crowd. John on the outside is an extrovert, but John on the inside is the exact opposite. He might even consider himself an introvert.

There are some people whose inner and outer aspects are aligned. But for most of us, there's quite a bit of complexity, and it's not easy to figure out exactly what a person needs in order to feel successful. How are we supposed to know this about a person without having to become an armchair psychologist?

RESPONSE BEHAVIOR

There's one last dimension that can gives you clues about how to connect with someone. When your inner needs are met, life is wonderful and you can easily adapt to what's thrown your way. But when these inner needs are not met, you react. By understanding a person's reaction to unmet needs, you can read the signals about how that person wants to be treated by you.

Let's take our example of John again. You see him sneaking out after the charity tournament without saying a word to anyone. That is now your signal of what John needs: time alone away from the crowd. So, knowing this, you can now anticipate what John needs and relate to him based on this characteristic.

If John is an important person to you, then you accommodate his inner needs by saying things like, "Hey, John, I know you're probably going to want to get home early rather than hanging around after this wraps up, so how about I contact you next week when you're back in your office?" It's not going to be effective to plan a business conversation at the 19th hole with John, who is only thinking about, "When can I get out of here?"

READING THE CLUES

Just by being observant, you can determine what your guest really needs but may not tell you. It's all about learning to read the signals of stress. Practice this until it becomes easy to you.

Here are some scenarios you might have even encountered already:

- When you see people losing energy, shutting down and becoming quiet and withdrawn, you can help bring them back by making sure no one embarrasses them, finding something positive to say, and creating a distraction to change the pace or focus until you see the energy return. Listen to them vent, but don't try to fix it. Just acknowledge the feelings. Only comment on the positive things they're doing and reassure them that their performance is not uncommon, that everyone has to deal with ups and downs.

- When you see people become overly tactical and take a lot of time measuring yardage and wind direction, and slipping into the paralysis of analysis, don't try to push them to make a decision. Help them get the information they need. In the process of collecting data, try to find a way to subtly lighten things up. Provide confirmation for their decisions so they move to action faster.

- When you're with people who become incredibly impatient with the pace of play or the results they're getting, and they react by pushing harder or even wrapping a club around a tree, realize that their restlessness will cause them to push harder and make decisions that will compound the problem. Pull them to the side and change their focus. Get them out of the moment and doing something else. Talk about a club in your bag that gives you trouble. Ask them direct questions about their equipment that requires them to respond with information. Give them something to do, like clean the club face or balls.

- When you're with people who become increasingly disorganized and impulsive, and you see them take unnecessary risks and look to place the blame on other people, the weather, or birds chirping in their back swing, they just aren't having enough fun. Create a strategic distraction by asking them in advance how they may play a shot so they get back in touch with the fundamentals rather than winging it. Try changing the mood by creating a contest that gets them focused on a particular shot, but keep it limited to a shot in the moment — something like closest to the current hole, not over an extended series of holes or shots, which may cause them to lose focus again.

Being able to recognize when strengths start to shift to stress is the secret weapon for knowing how to build a lasting relationship with a customer, client or prospect. (It also works for spouses, partners and kids!)

. . . .

 ## HOW TO KNOW WHAT'S IMPORTANT TO YOUR GUEST

READ THE BAG

- **If you see everything in place** …
  - o Be organized, review the rules, and let that person keep score. Watch your etiquette. Don't play out of turn.

- **If clubs are placed at random** …
  - o Don't ask this person to keep score. Be prepared to make concessions to the rules. Be ready to wager.

- **If this golfer has all the latest equipment and everything is high-performance** …
  - o Play the game with precision and speed. Keep the pace moving, and be prepared when it's your shot.

- **If the equipment is top-of-the-line but several years old** …
  - o Keep the pace relaxed, and let others play through if they're pushing. Don't pay too much attention to results.

OBSERVE BEHAVIOR ON THE PRACTICE RANGE

- **If there's a hurried and hectic warm-up with a variety of clubs** …
  - o Keep an eye out for clubs left behind and the possibility of missing the tee time.

- **If the person has a set warm-up routine and a consistent pre-shot procedure ...**
    - o Don't rush the pace or make this person tee off before he or she is ready.

- **If the person prefers to warm up alone out of the line of sight of people he or she may be playing with ...**
    - o Give people who do this plenty of space and time, and let them tell you when they are ready. Don't let them see you watching them practice.

- **If the warm-up looks like a routine at the gym — active and mainly pointed at distance clubs ...**
    - o Keep the practice time short and be ready to go when it's tee time.

WHILE YOU'RE PLAYING ON THE COURSE
- **If your guest makes frequent comments on the weather, the visuals of the course or the aesthetics ...**
    - o Keep things relaxed, and comments should always be positive and not necessarily about the round.

- **If your guest is continually studying the yardage book or a GPS device ...**
    - o Be observant of the rules and discuss strategy for playing a hole. Be prepared with local knowledge on how to play the course, if asked.

- **If the person is always going for distance, every par five is meant to be reached in two, and every hazard is an invitation to go for it ...**
    - o Applaud success and be ready when it's your turn to play. Keep the pace moving, and don't waste time looking for lost balls.

- **If your guest's constant conversation is interrupted only by occasional shots and the person is quick to offer advice about your swing or game ...**
    - o Be prepared with your own entertaining stories to tell. Use mulligans liberally, and go along with the banter and friendly wagers.

ON COURSE WITH ... PETER FOX
FOUNDING EXECUTIVE PRODUCER, ESPN

In 1976, I acquired the radio rights to broadcast from the PGA Tour's Sammy Davis Jr. Greater Hartford Open and hired golfing buddy Bill Rasmussen to anchor the coverage. He and my golfing mentor, J.R. Burrill, a protégé of Tommy Armour, were on the air and I produced content for them. It was a blast — and innovative.

Two summers later, Bill got fired from his Hartford Whalers play-by-play gig and he called me to ask this question: Do you think all-sports television will work? For this media, gym and golf course rat, it was an easy and loud YES!

Bill and his son had already begun to build what later would become ESPN and invited me to be its executive producer. My job was to put together a team of creative types who could develop content for the voracious appetite of a 24-hour sports channel.

Knowing what I know today, I would have a lot more hair and fewer recoveries if iMapMyTeam technology had been available to guide me.

There were some real dunderheads who made it through my flimsy recruiting practices. It all happened so incredibly fast — from our fledgling first demo-cast on November 17, 1978, to our official sign-on for round-the-clock sports on September 7, 1979. The crew that started as a handful of visionaries grew to hundreds overnight. Today it is thousands.

For an entity that glorified the heroics of teams, the organization's teams were chaotic, to be kind. The start-up attracted strong-minded people, many of whom, self-included, carted their cheering-has-stopped jock egos to work in wheelbarrows.

> *Knowing what I know today, I would have a lot more hair and fewer recoveries if iMapMyTeam technology had been available to guide me.*
>
> — Peter Fox,
> Founding Executive Producer,
> ESPN

Heaven help the bean counters — who ultimately won — when one of us sports junkies didn't get our way. Managers and marketers didn't fare much better in those fledgling moments — until the big money came along and shanghaied to ESPN a cadre of NBC executives who knew what they were doing.

Fast-forward a couple of decades and I was the pen-slinger hired to write and produce golf instruction for the company marketing the Moe Norman method of ball striking, where I met Connie Charles and her early iteration of iMapMyTeam, the incredible online software that would have helped me soothe the early ESPN savages.

I really admired her "guerilla tactics of using golf as bait" to introduce her true science to executives. Connie became renowned for making disparate workplace personalities get along and work well together, a formula she provided to the highest level at Fortune 100 companies.

When she hit a time and energy wall, she took a step back, bet the farm on putting her genius online so it became scalable, and voila: *www.iMapMyTeam.com.*

So let me ask you a question: Do you think there is an "I" in team? I do, and I wish there was then.

5

MASTER THE
FIVE-HOUR MEETING

It's supposed to be a fantastic day. The weather is perfect, the golf course is in tremendous shape, and you have everything set up at the course: tee time booked, caddies arranged, nothing left to chance. You're playing with a new client who is a decision-maker in the company, and it's going to be great.

Then the client shows up with no clubs and no shoes. No problem! You arrange for some rentals and head for the range to warm up. Your guest lets you know he is both excited to play your course, which he has heard so much about, and a little nervous because he hasn't touched a club in more than a year.

You beam, proud of your club's reputation as one of the most difficult in your area. Then, as you watch your client topping ball after ball, you begin to realize this might have been a mistake.

A mere six hours later you, are pulling away from the 18th green headed toward the clubhouse, and your guest is thoroughly humiliated. You are exhausted from searching the course for balls. Your client informs you that he needs to get going and doesn't have time for a drink at the 19th hole.

Congratulations — you have just become the worst golf experience your client has ever had. And the next call with him is, to say the least, uncomfortable.

This is a true story related to us by someone in one of our programs when we asked for people to share their best and worst stories from a golf experience. This is also a cautionary tale about how assumptions can get us in trouble.

In this case, the host assumed that inviting this client to his home club would be impressive and imagined it would strengthen the bond between them. The trouble was he didn't do his homework. With a little investigating, or by asking the right questions, the fact that this was a novice golfer would have been apparent and this day could have turned out much differently.

Even though you are very proud of your club, it might not be the best venue for every business golf experience. In this case, a business lunch and maybe a session on the driving range with some tips from your local professional could have resulted in a much better outcome.

THE FIVE-HOUR MEETING

Business golfers often refer to a round as "a five-hour meeting." That isn't meant to define how long you're on the golf course. Instead, it's meant to give you a sense of the time you should allocate to making sure the day is productive, effective and memorable.

As with all meetings, the devil is in the details. To have a successful meeting, you need a plan. Who should be in the meeting? Which venue would work best? What are the objectives? Remember, this isn't simply a casual game between friends. You need to orchestrate the experience from start to finish to be a true master of the five-hour meeting.

Part of the pre-game planning has to do with who you invite to your meeting. Are you after a decision-maker, an influencer, or a connector? This is important because who you are playing with will determine how you set up the meeting.

DETERMINE YOUR GUEST'S SKILL LEVEL

There are several details to be managed leading up to this round of business golf. For one thing, you must somehow determine the skill level of your partner. This is important when it comes to selecting the course you will play and the type of game you set up.

When we do a corporate program, we often use an icebreaker exercise at the beginning, having the participants share their best and worst golf experiences. Oftentimes the worst has something to do with having a humiliating experience at an event where the course was too demanding or the circumstances were too stressful. You don't want to be the subject of one of those "worst" experiences.

If you're a member of a private club, it's normal to take pride in and want to show off your home course. It's just a question of whether it is appropriate for the skill level of your playing partners. We suggest you have more than one course in your network of business golf venues: something easy for the less-skilled golfers to offset the more demanding courses for the more-seasoned golfers.

KNOW THE STAFF AT THE COURSE

Whatever the venue, you should know the course well — not only the physical layout, so you can be the "caddy," sharing local knowledge such as yardages, greens reading, hazard placement, and those sorts of facts. You should also form a close relationship with all of the service staff at the course. From the staff members outside who greet the guests and handle their golf bags, to the inside staff in the golf shop who register the players, to the restaurant staff serving the drinks, to the starter at the first tee, these people should be thought of as an extension of your workplace support staff. You should know them by name and they should know you, and they should know who your guests are so they can help facilitate the perfect day.

These people can be invaluable in creating an impressive experience, so take care of them when it comes to tipping. The staff can also cover for you if (and we want to stress this should never happen) something prevents you from getting to the course ahead of your guests. You don't want your client feeling like a stranger in a strange land. Your relationship with the staff members will allow them to cover for you until you arrive.

SET UP THE PERFECT EXPERIENCE

So you know who you are playing with and you know that guest's skill level, and you've chosen a venue that's appropriate. What's next? To orchestrate the day, you need to book the tee time. Make sure you allow enough time before you tee off to warm up at the range. Let your guests know to arrive early.

You should also ask guests ahead of time what brand of ball they prefer so you can have a couple of sleeves ready for them when you head to the first tee. Feel out the kind of game you're going to play. Better players will want to play their own ball and probably keep score either with or without handicaps. Less-skilled players may enjoy a "scramble" or a type of game that takes some of the pressure off of them.

Another important decision to be made is what tee boxes to use. You might be a good player and prefer to play from the tips. But you should keep in mind that this day is not about you. You can observe your playing partners on the range and figure out what tee box will be appropriate, or simply ask them what they usually do. And don't assume that if you're playing with a woman, she will automatically play from the forward tees. A number of very good women players prefer to start from the men's tees. Assumptions like that can get you off to a rough start.

Just remember, the quality of the day — and the effectiveness of the five-hour meeting you are arranging — depends on the five P's: Prior planning prevents poor performance. Taking time to plan the details on the front end will allow you and your guests to enjoy the experience together, and maybe that will lead to good things off the course.

ON COURSE WITH ... BENITA FORTNER
DIRECTOR, SUPPLIER DIVERSITY, RAYTHEON

Why I play golf: I actually started later in life, and since then I've been smacking myself in the head saying, "What took you so long?" I'm a pretty good athlete and can pick up almost any sport. I spent a lot of time playing tennis or bowling. I actually had a very negative experience with golf and it was because I didn't play. I had been contacted by a headhunter for a position that was perfect for me. The interview process went smoothly and I was verbally offered the job. It was right before Thanksgiving and I was told I would get the formal offer as soon as people got back to the office on the following Monday. I went into the holiday really excited about this new direction only to get to Monday and no phone call. No offer. Finally the headhunter called and said they had withdrawn the offer. Apparently over the long weekend, the CEO was playing golf with a person who had done some work for him and now needed a job. Magically, my offer went away.

> " *I was able to get people to do what I needed by attaching a round of golf to the request.*
>
> — Benita Fortner, Director, Supplier Diversity, Raytheon "

How golf has helped me in business: Although it took me awhile to get into the game, once I learned its power, I was hooked. I learned how big my sphere of influence became by bringing a leader into the company just by offering to play golf. I was able to get people to do what I needed by attaching a round of golf to the request. It also became the great neutralizer. Conversation on the course humanized people that I might otherwise have had difficulty working with. It created a bond around the mutual thing we both enjoyed and enabled us to be more open about other things.

How golf has made me more self-aware: Golf is the most humbling game. After 15 years of playing, I'm still not that great, and I'm a reasonable athlete. It helps me look at parts of myself the way others see me. It forces me to manage my type A personality so that I learn to be quiet and the determination turns into relaxation. The ball actually flies better when I'm relaxed and not trying so hard. That's a difficult lesson for those of us who are driven to smash everything.

Advice for budding golfers: Learn to play golf now. But don't get confused by playing golf and being a good golfer. Understand what you need to know to be on the playing field. Learn the rules so you know how the game unfolds. And most of all, find a way to make it fun. People evaluate you based on how it is to be with you for four hours, not on what you scored. Accept poor performance graciously and don't pile your disappointment onto other people. They don't want to see your negative reactions. It also applies to how you react when you're performing well. How are you to be with either way? Accept your performance as it is and enjoy the company you're with.

6

THE BUSINESS CASE FOR CORPORATE INVESTMENT

Golf is different from any other sport. When professional golfers make a mistake in play, they call "foul" on themselves, even when no one else is watching. The game's built-in rules and etiquette rely on the basic tenets of integrity, honesty, respect and discipline — values that align with the vision and mission of most organizations. This is just one reason golf and business go together so well.

But why should corporations, small companies, professional firms and individuals make the game of golf a part of their business strategy? The reason is simple. The sport provides a return on investment like no other.

There's no question you can make a difference as an individual getting involved in golf. The game can help you meet the right people who can influence your career path and speed your ascent up the corporate ladder. Many successful people credit the game with their rise to the top. Being a skilled golfer opens doors and presents opportunities otherwise not available.

We've heard countless stories of the networking value of playing golf and the amazing business relationships that were forged during a round. And there is no better way to evaluate someone you might be considering for a role in your company than a four-hour interview conducted over 18 holes of golf.

But how can you convince your organization that it's a good idea to get involved in golf on a bigger scale?

If you're in a leadership position, there are all kinds of ways to begin establishing golf awareness in your organization. Sponsor a golf event. Your local PGA section is always looking for tournament sponsors and can help you leverage the opportunity. You can also sponsor or participate in charity events, with members of your team getting involved in organizing, playing, volunteering and supporting.

You can encourage employees to start playing by setting up learning opportunities, enlisting a local pro to conduct group clinics. And you can make sure employees who already play are given opportunities to go out on the course with existing or potential clients.

Golf is continuing to grow in popularity, and one of the most exciting aspects is the inroads it's making with youths, young adults and women. In an April 2015 article in *Forbes* magazine, the commissioner of the Ladies Professional Golf Association expressed it this way: "We have entered an exciting time in the industry — the age of full "inclusion" — where attracting/accepting more people … is no longer just a talking point, but an actionable reality across the board."

The game's charitable impact is about $4 billion a year through 143,000 events and 12 million participants, the article said. Golf raises more money for charity than the combined contributions of Major League Baseball, the National Basketball Association, the National Football League and the National Hockey League. Again, this fits into the mission of most corporations, which realize the importance of giving back to the community through efforts such as United Way fund drives. Golf offers another avenue for achieving that goal.

Another sign: The PGA Tour has signed unprecedented long-term deals with corporate sponsors — 20 years with financial services firm Charles Schwab and 10 years with insurance firm Travelers and trash disposal company Waste Management. For conservative organizations to invest in the future of the game, they must see the ROI of associating their brands with the sport.

Here are some observations from Dave, who has a front-row seat to see how golf and corporate sponsorship work hand in hand:

BUSINESS GOLF EXPERIENCE

Throughout my long career in the golf industry, I have often been included in what we are describing in this book as business golf. During my playing career, I participated in pro-am events that featured corporate sponsors paired up with one of the professionals playing in that particular week's PGA Tour event. Usually held on the Wednesday before the official start of the tournament, these pro-am events gave the sponsors a way to connect with the golf pros and to reward employees or entertain key clients by getting the chance to get "inside the ropes."

The experience for the corporate representatives was often as terrifying as it was exciting. Most of them had never played golf in front of more people than their usual foursome. I spent a great deal of my time helping them to keep calm, maybe giving them a swing tip or two, and hunting for the occasional ball in the bushes.

Eventually, after they got over the initial shock of being in the spotlight, I would try to shift the conversations to how they got involved with the tournament and what they were hoping to get out of it. By the end of the round, I would inevitably be asked to drop by their corporate tent to meet others in their organization and perhaps some of their clients. More often than not I obliged, which led to me cementing relationships I still have today.

These experiences also laid the foundation for my lifelong fascination with what compels people to play this game … especially business people.

After my playing career, I began to focus on teaching the game and started a golf school. Through the school, I came in contact with some of the same executives I had played with in those pro-am events. Now their goal was to improve their golf skills, and in this five-day immersive program they certainly accomplished that. But I would find myself asking them the same question: "What do you hope to get out of this?"

For some of them, it was to become better as a golfer so they would get more satisfaction and enjoyment from the game. For others, though, it was a strategic decision to be able to use the game as a way to achieve business objectives.

This was a turning point for me — and also an opportune time to be introduced to Connie. What followed was collaboration between us and the myriad executives looking for ways to combine the game with a business objective.

We still work with many of these companies today because they recognize the opportunities the game presents. Some of these companies use the game to build stronger connections with their clients. There's a saying that you can learn more about a person in one round of golf than you can in 100 hours of meetings. The typical business meeting is orchestrated, predictable and usually emotionally guarded. The golf course experience, on the other hand, is unpredictable, more spontaneous, and often emotionally revealing.

HOW TO DETERMINE ROI

So how do you take advantage of the benefits this great game can provide and justify the investment in both dollars and time? From where I stand, it's easy to do.

A number of members at my club regularly bring clients out to play as a way to strengthen the relationship, or potential clients to give them an experience that might help close a deal. I am sometimes asked to play along to help with local knowledge like reading greens and confirming yardages.

What I witness during these rounds is the absolute bonding that can take place in this shared experience. Those adept at this create such loyalty with clients that the investment in time is easily justified.

One business golfer I know invites vendors to play as guests at charity events. It accomplishes a couple of things: He gets to support a favorite cause and write off the expense, and he gets to spend several hours with the vendors in an environment that allows plenty of time to softly negotiate contracts or talk about upcoming needs. Most of these kinds of events are scrambles, where people play as a team and hit from the best shot. These keep the pressure off and give everyone an opportunity to shine.

For those of you who can't seem to find the time to get out to the course during work hours, you can still reap some of the benefits. One of the new developments in golf is the entertainment complex Topgolf. This takes the old driving range concept and turns it on its head. There is a golf element to it, but not in a conventional way. It's kind of like a giant video game played with golf balls with chips in them and targets with sensors in them. The technology allows all kinds of different games to be played for competition or just for fun.

This is combined with a vibrant nightclub scene with a restaurant, a bar and ample room for socializing. Topgolf also caters to the corporate crowd with private conference rooms as well as meeting space with all of the necessities like AV equipment. They even have special sections on the tee line that can be reserved for a corporate function. This gives even the novice business golfer a way to at least dip a toe in the water and have a golf experience with a client or colleague. *See Chapter 15: Golf Alternatives* for more ideas.

UNDERSTANDING THE INVESTMENT

People express all kinds of reasons golf might not be a valuable investment for business: It takes too much time and is too expensive. Shareholders will view it as frivolous spending. It's too difficult to track your organization's ROI. And for those who don't understand how to effectively use the game in the way we outline in this book, these reasons are probably correct.

But history has proved that golf is a solid investment. Don't just take our word for it. Next time you watch a professional event on TV, whether it's the PGA Tour, the LPGA Tour or the Champions Tour, pay attention to the title sponsor's name and listen to the on-air interview with the company representative who explains why it is such a good fit for the organization to be investing in the event. Or look at the corporate logos on the shirts, hats and golf bags of the tournament players.

If you're lucky enough to have one of these tour events in your community, go spend a day and talk to the people staffing the corporate tents throughout the course, and you will start to get an idea of why this connection between golf and business is not only viable but essential.

We believe golf has played a significant role in the world's economic rebound. Corporate sponsorship of all professional tour events is at unprecedented levels, producing record purses and shattering charitable contributions.

We are seeing the same commitment to the game within and outside of the United States. Golf is continuing to grow on a global scale, with participation increasing in most developed countries. In fact, the largest golf resort in the world is located outside of Schenzhen, China. Mission Hills has a dozen 18-hole golf courses and three golf schools with their own private practice facilities. In 2004, it surpassed Pinehurst resort in the United States as the largest golf facility in the world as ranked by the *Guinness Book of World Records*. Each of its courses was designed by a different golf personality, creating lots of opportunity for diverse playing experiences. I was there for one of their international tournaments a few years ago and it was amazing to see the place up close and personal.

The resort that supplements play at my private club has seen a surge in business and leisure bookings from Europe and Asia in the past couple of years. So while we here in the U.S. deal with that age-old economics formula of supply and demand, the future is bright as far as we're concerned.

HISTORY OF BUSINESS GOLF INVESTING

Decades ago, the National Cash Register company had its own golf course, built as an employee perk. It offered recreation for employees, as well as a place for them to entertain clients and hold meetings in a nonbusiness environment while staying inside the gates of the company.

In the early days of professional golf, you saw very few players on the tours wearing corporate logos. The Amana kitchen appliance company started giving the players hats with its corporate logo and awarding them prizes every time they were shown on camera wearing them. This started a trend of sponsoring players and eventually morphed into sponsoring tournaments.

In those days, Hollywood entertainers were the sponsors, including Sammy Davis Jr., Glen Campbell, Dean Martin, Bing Crosby, Bob Hope. Entertainers lent their names to give the game a push, and then you started to see under the title "Brought to you by" and a logo for Chevrolet, Ford, Penzoil and other "title sponsors."

Corporations came to understand that the demographic of the golf fan base was a perfect match with that of their ideal customers. Today pro golfers don't quite rival NASCAR drivers in the number of logos they display on their clothing or equipment, but they are coming close. Numerous corporations across industries have put their brands on the sport and its individual players, and an increase in golf-related TV shows has helped them boost their exposure.

Organizations invest in golf today for numerous reasons, not all of them as easy to quantify as the salesperson's ability to attribute a new contract directly to a relationship built on the course. Some of the benefits are less tangible. Corporations sponsor events that raise money for charity, and having their name attached to those events spreads goodwill among potential customers. Golf allows strategic partnerships to form, which spurs businesses on to larger projects that bring in more revenue.

As with any endeavor, you get out of it what you put into it. Using golf as a corporate business tool, and tracking its ROI for your organization, can take some work. But the benefits will pay off in very real ways.

ON COURSE WITH ... ANNE TOULOUSE
CORPORATE VICE PRESIDENT, GLOBAL BRAND MANAGEMENT AND ADVERTISING, BOEING

Why I play golf: First of all, I love being outdoors. Having grown up in Florida, I take any opportunity to be outside. I also am very competitive and like being active. I have a philosophical view that everyone should choose a sport to play for life. I was really pleased when my son chose golf as his sport. When I was a girl, I used to drive my grandmother's golf cart and got to go to the ladies' luncheon with her afterward, which I thought was pretty cool.

How I started: I first got started playing golf when I was a civilian office assistant in the U.S. Air Force. My supervisor, who was also a woman, insisted that I learn how to play if I was going to be in business. She gave me an old set of clubs that were a mixture of men's and women's, so I had to choke down on the shaft because they were way too long. She took me out my first time and made sure I stuck with the game.

How golf has made me more self-aware: Golf reminds me that being in the moment delivers results that are so much better. I bring my best to the table when I'm in the moment, paying attention to my breathing in my back swing and being conscious of when I exhale. Recovery is key. You can focus on what just happened, but that's not going to get you anywhere in the moment. Talk about what happened later. In the moment, you have to focus on what you're going to do to recover, whether it be from a bad shot or from a business decision that's not working out. Save the reflecting for later.

How golf has helped me develop business relationships: Every year, Boeing has a leadership meeting with all of its executives, and golf is one of

> *You get to talk about so many other things and ask questions that you never get a chance to ask in a business setting.*
>
> — Anne Toulouse, Corporate Vice President, Global Brand Management and Advertising, Boeing

51

the activities you can choose. I always play because it's a way to reach out beyond my function into other parts of the organization. This shared experience of golf gives you insight about somebody that you don't get when you're sitting across the table at a company dinner or in a meeting. You get to talk about so many other things and ask questions that you never get a chance to ask in a business setting. The first year I played in this event, I was paired with another executive and we were both beginners. We had a great time playing "best ball" and even played a few extra holes. Even though that was a great relationship-building event, what really impressed me was when I met up with him again a year later, he had turned into an amazing golfer. It was obvious that he spent a lot of time working on his game, and it was a reminder to me that what you focus on you can accomplish. We all have really big jobs and schedules that are crazy, but he focused, and the results showed it.

Advice for people thinking of taking up golf: The advice that was given to me, which I pass along, is first of all get lessons. Second, don't be fearful. You have to get out on the course. And lastly, enjoy it. It has business value and is your way to connect with people.

7

COMPETING ON A GLOBAL SCALE

It's easy today to conduct business in other parts of the world, no matter where you live and work. News reports help us stay informed, travel options help us meet face to face, and the Internet helps us stay connected. Why is all of this important in golf? Because golf is a language that is recognized all over the globe. The skills you pick up through the game can help you deal with cultural differences anywhere you go. We'll let Connie tell you her story here:

My interest in all things global started when I was very young. In their late 20s, my parents decided to uproot their family of five children and move from the United States to Peru to pursue their calling to save the world. I was nine when they arrived in Lima.

Because I learned the language quickly, my parents gave me free rein to wander the city on my own or with my brother in tow. I developed street smarts that enabled me to navigate between rich and poor and among a wide variety of cultures. This early start in life made me comfortable with ethnic diversity and has also fueled my insatiable desire to get on a plane to some distant land.

When I first launched my firm in 1990, with great aspiration I added the word "International" to its name. I knew I wanted to conduct business around the globe. This vision has resulted in projects and opportunities from the United Kingdom to Singapore and beyond.

Although my early life set the stage for a fascination with international business, my work in corporate America gave me insight into what makes doing business in different cultures so challenging. This is especially true when negotiating contracts, establishing partnership agreements or attempting anything competitive that requires deal-making. There's a fundamentally different approach to competitiveness that can breed mistrust and ultimately the loss of business when it's misunderstood.

MEASURING COMPETITIVENESS

In our corporate work, we start by collecting data on each person who is part of the business team. Participants answer a 30-minute questionnaire, which produces a profile that describes four dimensions of their behavior: strengths, passions, motivational needs, and reactions under stress. There is one data point that evaluates competitiveness, and it is here that we find an amazing difference between cultures. The competitive profile of a North American business person, on average, is different from that of someone brought up in another culture.

To illustrate this point, take this brief quiz to see where you fall on the scale. Check the boxes next to the statements that most fit the way you manage a competitive situation or opportunity.

• •

 # HOW DO YOU COMPETE?

MY STRENGTHS WHEN COMPETING ARE:

☐ TRUST OTHER PEOPLE   ☐ OPPORTUNITY MINDED
☐ COOPERATIVE   ☐ FOCUS ON WINNING
☐ WELL-MEANING   ☐ GOOD AT NEGOTIATING
☐ LOYAL   ☐ FORCEFUL

WHEN IN A COMPETITIVE SITUATION, I EXPECT:

☐ FAIRNESS   ☐ INDIVIDUAL INCENTIVES
☐ MUTUAL TRUST   ☐ COMPETITIVE ADVANTAGE
☐ TEAM COLLABORATION   ☐ ACHIEVEMENTS RECOGNIZED
☐ SHARED SUCCESS   ☐ TO WIN

WHEN A COMPETITIVE SITUATION IS NOT GOING WELL, I CAN BECOME:

☐ GULLIBLE   ☐ SELF PROMOTIONAL
☐ IMPRACTICAL   ☐ OPPORTUNISTIC

This isn't a scientifically validated questionnaire and relies on your own self-awareness to be in any way accurate. However, it will give you some ideas about the different types of behavior that can be seen in competitive situations.

If you checked more boxes on the left side of the questionnaire, then you could be somewhat of an idealist. You place an emphasis on fairness, and ultimately winning is the result of being better than anyone else at what you do. You probably keep your distance when the negotiations get heated and may find that you end up giving more than the other party just to take the high road and be fair. You respond well to causes that are linked to your personal values, and these could be more important than actually winning.

If you checked more boxes on the right side, then you may find yourself to be competitive on lots of levels. You like having a scoreboard that tells you how well you're doing as well as clear rules or requirements for what it takes to win. The worst thing that can happen is if someone changes those rules or doesn't come through with the rewards even though you've met the standards. Although you can compete as a member of a team, you really like knowing how you personally can win and may find yourself looking for ways to excel more than your colleagues. You love to negotiate, bargain for what you want and manage the competitive playing field so that you have an advantage.

Now, why is this important? The profile of most people living in North America matches the first description. That's what the data shows. However, when you get outside of North America, the data changes significantly, and there are more people whose behavior matches the second description. So anytime you get in competitive situations on an international level, often Americans are at a disadvantage because they are playing with a different rulebook than the rest of the world. This is a serious issue for North American companies that are looking to expand globally as well as the competitive golf tournaments that are increasingly drawing players from around the world.

THE SECRET TO WINNING

The solution is not to change who we are and how we've learned to compete. Instead, it's learning to be conscious of the competitive landscape and deliberately making choices that come from both ends of the spectrum of behaviors. If you see that making this change in your approach is linked to your ability to win, you'll find the motivation you need to make those changes. You are who you are, but if you want to be successful in a wider variety of competitive situations, you need to learn to manage your behaviors in order to gain the competitive advantage.

The other part of competitiveness is to make sure you've defined the "win." If you're playing golf with a prospective customer, the win may not be claiming the best score at the end of the round but instead gaining a new contract to do business. Sometimes great golfers think the round is all about the game and forget there is a higher purpose. Reading the signals your client gives can help you decide what type of competitor you need to be in that specific round of golf.

If your playing partner is constantly focused on the score, making side bets, and spending little time talking about anything other than the round, you are probably up against someone who is not playing just for fun. Even if your golf skills are not as good, play for the win — even if it's just that hole or a particular shot. Find a way to win little "battles" and you'll gain more respect because you gave it your best shot.

If you're playing with someone who doesn't track the score, can't remember what each of you shot on a particular hole, and takes multiple mulligans, this person might be more open to developing the relationship than on winning. In this case, a good round of golf is not defined by your score at the end of the 18th hole. It's defined by the camaraderie built with those playing, the beauty of the course and a relaxed approach to play.

In using golf for business purposes, you need to start by defining your win. Know what "prize" you're really after. Then manage your way through the round by responding to the competitive nature of the other person. Master this and you'll achieve your goals.

COMPETING FOR THE RYDER CUP

The Ryder Cup gives us a snapshot of these characteristics played out in a golf tournament. Historically, the United States has not done well in the team portion of the competition. That's because U.S. golfers are all playing as individuals and they don't pull it together until it's only their performance that matters. It makes sense because this is all they are used to.

The European team, on the other hand, knows that to win a team competition, you have to act like a team. This takes a special type of preparation. The Europeans take more measures to ensure they will win. They know it takes more than just showing up ready to play your best game of golf. The Europeans put effort into being a team. They travel as a group, eat meals together and get to know each other outside of their professional experiences. They work hard to build the relationships so they can maximize the power of the team.

This is a good example of managing the competitive playing field by taking charge and ensuring you've done everything in your power to win. We even see a different personality when the Europeans are in the Ryder Cup than when they're playing as individuals. They've learned to set aside their natural approach to competition, which places the spotlight on their personal performance. The Americans keeps playing their same game and don't know how to switch to a different strategy.

Whether you're competing for someone's time and attention, your next big deal, the club championship or even the Ryder Cup, the key to winning is to understand your approach to competition and then modify your behavior so you have more tools in your bag to help you win. And if your competitor is from a different part of the globe, be prepared to come up against new competitive rules that may be foreign to you. Become aware of your own competitive drivers as well as those of your companions so you can manage the pathway to a win.

ON COURSE WITH ... MARK HARDAKER
PRESIDENT, TRIOMADA PLASTIC INTERNATIONAL CO. LTD.
KINGDOM OF BAHRAIN

Why I play golf: I don't play golf as often as I might. One reason might be that I live in a sand trap, a rather large one albeit, called Bahrain in the Arabian Gulf, where water and greenery are at a premium. We have a difficult course here at the Royal Bahrain Golf Club: long, narrow, unforgiving, and in the summer very hot.

It wasn't always like that. I started playing golf in the early 1980s with a business buddy of mine in Leighton Buzzard in the UK. He was a moderate golfer and persuaded me that I should pick up a club and hit some balls around the local municipal public course there. Of course, I loved it, even though I was less than majestic those first few outings. Over time, I quickly realized that any concept of playing "against" someone else doesn't work in golf — you are playing against yourself the whole time. Don't have a bad day in the office and hope to take out those bad feeling on the ball on the course in the afternoon. It just makes you feel worse!

How golf has helped me in business: Golf is not generally a sport that brings people together in the Middle East. We have few good-quality courses — except, of course, in Dubai — and few locals play the game. However, golf has always been useful to building relationships with consultants, distributors and agents in faraway lands. I will never forget the first time I hit an eagle while on a business trip to Nigeria. We were scheduled to meet up with a local oil company to discuss possible consulting solutions and decided that the pace of discussion required a change of scenery.

Repairing to the local golf course, we discovered it was generally old and unkempt. It had "browns," not "greens." The intensity of the discus-

> *Golf requires the same skills you need in business: tenacity, self-control and the dogged determination not to give up at the first hurdle.*
>
> — Mark Hardaker, President, Triomada Plastic International Co. Ltd.

sions intensified still further as we went around the course, made only more stressful for me by being on an unknown course with impossible raked-sand putting greens.

On the back nine, the temperature — in both my temper and the climate — was reaching a peak, until the 14th hole. From the tee box, I lashed out at the ball, thumping it and slicing it badly into the trees to the right. A loud thud was heard, a muffled squawk, and — yes — a startled gray eagle fell out of the tree onto the ground below. I was sure I'd killed it, but it recovered, dusted itself off and, after a couple of seconds, took off into the air, no doubt vowing never to venture near a golf course again! Of course, the tension of the day evaporated immediately and we laughed all the way back to the clubhouse. To this day, that is the one and only eagle I've hit on a golf course. And we did get the business, by the way.

The warmth of friendships established in business, coupled with the level playing field you are on in an outside environment away from the phones and email, helps to build trust and friendship and an atmosphere where deals can be done.

How golf has made me more self-aware: There are few sports where self-discipline is more important than in golf. In team sports, you can sometimes hide poor performance temporarily behind your teammates. In squash, tennis or badminton, your opponent may actually be physically better and stronger than you. But in golf, it's really you against you, with the other players on your team or your opponents coming along for the ride. How you conduct yourself, how you handle the internally generated frustration of a badly hit drive, or a missed two-foot putt, determines how the others regard you and your likelihood of going on to win. Golf requires the same skills you need in business: tenacity, self-control and the dogged determination not to give up at the first hurdle. The ability to calm yourself under pressure, not to react and throw your metaphorical clubs in the lake (have you seen it done?), but to reload and try again. The desire to try a new direction, learning from the mistakes you make.

How golf has helped me develop business relationships: The thing about our local Bahrain course is that it makes for a convenient love-triangle. It's you, me and the course. Two of us are vulnerable, thirsty, hot and tired; the other is constant, unchanging and unforgiving. So it's not surprising that you have an immediate bond with anyone you play with here. After the initial "What the heck is this course you've brought me to", a warm bond of friendship quickly forms as the battle to complete the round continues under the hot sun. It's in just these conditions that business relationships can develop and mature.

Advice for novices: My first advice is to be sure your partner is understanding about the immense lifestyle change you are about to make. Golf can require as much love and commitment as you give to your spouse — more, in many cases. If she or he is unwilling to accept you playing in tournaments, you probably shouldn't start. I would also counsel starting small and building up to the game. Don't go out and buy the most expensive gear just to look good on the course. What counts is how your golf looks and, more important, how you behave on the course. I have a good friend in Bahrain who dresses the part, has the best clubs, hits a massive drive and putts for dough. Unfortunately, if he loses or merely has a bad day, he breaks his clubs, throws them in the air, shouts, swears and curses. It's important to learn to be calm and gentlemanly (or womanly?) at all times.

8

ASSESS YOUR OWN SKILL

We are often asked whether skill matters when it comes to business golf, and our answer is a resounding ... maybe. It all depends on the kind of golf experience you intend to use as part of your strategy. You certainly don't need to be a low handicap to be able to play and be an effective host.

This is where we introduce you to what we call the Business Golf Handicap. Your BGH isn't the measure of how you score relative to par. Rather, it's the measure of your skills and abilities to plan, execute and leverage a business golf experience. We know several people who'd be the equivalent of scratch players at business golf who can barely break 90 on the course. What they lack in physical skills they more than make up for in the fine art of facilitating an experience.

• •

 ## HANDICAP SYSTEM

A long time ago, someone came up with the bright idea of establishing a handicap system. The United States Golf Association (USGA) developed the system, which celebrated its 100th anniversary in 2001 and is still in use today. It was designed to create a level playing field between golfers of varying ability so they could compete against each other in a fair way.

In essence, a better player has a lower handicap while a less-skilled player has a higher handicap. If a 7 handicap plays against a 14 handicap, the 14 gets to subtract 1 stroke from his or her score on the 7 toughest holes as rated on the scorecard.

Each hole on a course is rated according to length and difficulty, and it's assigned a handicap rating between 1 (the most difficult) and 18 (the least difficult). The system has been tweaked over the years to take into account how one course compares to another in relative difficulty, a measurement known as the "slope system." You can usually find a course's slope rating listed on the scorecard according to the various tee positions someone plays. There is a full explanation of this system and how to go about establishing a handicap at www.USGA.org.

We strongly suggest you do what is necessary to acquire a handicap. First of all, it shows you're serious enough to do the work. Second, it provides a way for a variety of skill levels to play together.

. . . .

People with a great BGH can play with very skilled golfers and never seem to get in the way. They know how to keep the pace of the round at the perfect speed and how to make everyone in the group feel comfortable. They know how to make sure their guests feel at ease from the time they arrive at the venue until they reach the 19th hole.

So let's look at the criteria necessary for a scratch Business Golf Handicap. The first measure is your golf skill level. If you are a 0-18 handicap, you can play with anyone and make a good impression as a golfer. If you are a 19 or higher handicap, you might want to review *Chapter 15: Golf Alternatives* and consider some other golf-related activities instead of 18 holes of play.

Next is how well you know those you've invited to share the experience. The more you know about them, the better you will be equipped to create the optimal experience. Matching the experience with the person can take a little research to discover personal interests, preferred activities, situations to avoid and other factors. But that research can pay enormous benefits.

Your familiarity with the venue you choose to use also plays into your BGH. You don't want to experiment when you are the host. Take the time to not only visit the location but get to know the staff, the physical layout, the best times to be there and anything else you can discover about the venue. Take the element of surprise out of the equation so you can focus on your guests and your objective.

ON COURSE WITH ... STEDMAN GRAHAM
CHAIRMAN AND CEO, S. GRAHAM & ASSOCIATES

Why I play golf: My introduction to golf was when I was about 13 or 14 years old and my brother and some friends were caddies at the local country club. I don't think I was very good because I was always the last to be picked. And I was always paid the minimum, which was 50 cents a bag, and you carried two bags. The others were getting 75 cents a bag, and I thought it was unbelievable that you could make a dollar-fifty! Because of segregation, we weren't allowed to play, so we would just take old balls and clubs and practice hitting shots across the railroad tracks. Then we'd have to go find them all so we could hit again. But I have great golf memories from those early days in New Jersey.

How golf has helped me in business: I wouldn't be here today talking with you if it weren't for golf. It was Bob Brown who officially introduced me to the game. He had a trip to Africa planned and asked me if I played golf. I told him that I did play, so I got invited to join this trip. When we got to Africa, he asked me where my bag was. Now what he didn't understand was that I said I played golf based on my experience of hitting balls across a railroad track. I didn't know you needed to have your own clubs because I had never actually played on a golf course.

> " *You have to be patient. Golf teaches you discipline. Most of all, it teaches you about others' personalities.*
>
> — Stedman Graham, Chairman and CEO, S. Graham & Associates "

Well, Bob was very gracious and got me set up, and I became dedicated to the game and practiced as much as I could. He was also the owner of Pinehurst, and I started working for him. He would invite a lot of business people to play, so over the years I made many friends and business associates as a result of those introductions. I credit most of my success to golf.

How golf has made me more self-aware: You have to be patient. Golf teaches you discipline. Most of all, it teaches you about others' personalities. As you play more, you watch people who are role models for behavior. You get to spend the whole day with a teacher.

Advice for budding golfers: Make sure you take lessons. They don't have to be expensive. Develop a library and learn as much as you can about the game, and practice as often as you can. Skill is in the ability to prepare.

9

MENTAL MULLIGAN

You practice, you plan, you think you're prepared, and then you get surprised by something unexpected. It's perfectly natural for you to hit your stress behavior in those moments when everything falls apart. You start slicing the ball, your shot ends up in the water, it's raining, the client is late for the tee time. All of these could be the trigger for a meltdown.

We call it the stairway to golfing hell. It starts with something that gets you off balance. Your behavior begins to move from in control to out of control. You react to the situation with behaviors that can often bring on unintended consequences. And if that first step, minor in and of itself, is followed by a second surprise and then a third or fourth, you can find yourself in golfing hell, totally out of control and not getting the result you want.

Your tee shot goes into the woods and you lose your ball. This could lead to missing the putt, which then leads to a poor tee shot on the next hole. So one bad shot turns into a bad hole, which turns into a bad front nine, and if you carry the stress with you into the back nine, you end up playing a bad round. If this happens often enough, your clubs go into long-term storage.

This could be particularly damaging if you're playing with a client. Because, as we all know, sometimes the round is not about golf but about an assessment of your character and whether or not someone wants to do business with you.

It's an undeniable fact that golf can be a really cruel game some days, and even your good shots can end up in a creek. These challenges can either make us or break us. How you handle yourself when your performance is off or you're trying to manage conditions that are out of your control is noted by your playing partners and may make the difference in whether or not they continue a relationship with you.

One of the most important life lessons you can learn on the golf course is how to manage yourself when you are under stress. Mastering this will tee you up for success in any situation, personal or professional. Self-control is your way of conquering the unexpected when you have no control over outside circumstances.

Just like a mulligan in golf, it's a do-over, a chance to start fresh. The Mental Mulligan is designed to help you gain quick recovery when you start to feel the turn in your behavior from in control to out of control, or a reaction. This response is involuntary when you feel you have minimal control over the situation. It's like if someone makes a loud noise six inches from your face. It's impossible to control the natural reaction of jumping or at least blinking.

We all are wired to react to stressful situations with predictable responses to circumstances out of our control. Let's look at illustrations of four reactions and suggestions for a Mental Mulligan that will offset the stress reactions and help you regain control more quickly. These are an antidote for those stress behaviors and will ensure that you quickly get back on track.

BARRY — EMBARRASSED IN PUBLIC

Barry is sensitive about how other people react to his performance on the golf course. It's usually hardest for him on the tee box, where everyone's eyes are on him as he hits the ball. The nervousness he feels often results in a poor tee shot because he starts worrying that he's going to hit a bad shot and then delivers on his negative thinking.

If he's playing business golf, he feels even more pressure to perform because there's more at stake than just a round of golf. Because of this, he may overthink shots as he tries to get the "feel" of a good swing back. He may spend more time off to the side with a club in his hand hitting a blade of grass. Or, when it is his turn to hit his ball he may take more than the usual number of practice swings before he actually addresses the ball.

If Barry starts playing poorly, or if someone makes what he would perceive as critical remark, he may start to shut down, avoid people, and even look for ways to not have to continue the round. He may feel embarrassed and start to withdraw from conversation. He may try to hide his feelings from the others in the foursome, but on the inside he's a bundle of nerves.

In order to avoid the any negative consequences from these behaviors, Barry's Mental Mulligan might be:

- Just do it
- Action
- Think, don't feel
- Pick up the pace

REBECCA — READY TO ROLL

Rebecca is all about speed and action. She can get terribly frustrated by a foursome ahead of her whose pace of play is causing her to wait. She expects people to make quick decisions about things like choice of club or whether or not to lay up or to go for the green. Her best rounds are ones that are played in less than three hours, and anything that gets in the way of that will cause her to become impatient and insensitive to the things or people that slow her down.

Additionally, Rebecca relishes the big shots, so things like how far she hits a ball or whether or not she outdrives the others in her foursome matter to her. If her game is off and she's slicing the ball, hitting worm burners, or even whiffing a shot, her anger can bubble to the surface and become highly visible to other people. It may not be uncommon to see her bang the ground (or a nearby tree) with her club, utter some expletive or drive the cart at a precarious pace. If others are causing the slowdown in play, she may even do something to put pressure on them to play faster, like hit into their foursome.

In order to avoid the consequences of these behaviors when Rebecca starts to have those types of experience, she would benefit from these Mental Mulligans:

- Deep breath
- Smell the flowers
- Take a chill pill
- Relax
- Focus on rhythm

GARY — GAMBLE ON A WIN

Gary is everyone's friend, and when he shows up at the club he instantly transforms it into a party. He would never consider playing by himself because he draws energy from other people and always plays his best when he is having fun with his playing partners. He also likes to win and will set up opportunities to compete openly with his foursome and may even find a way to stack the deck. All in good fun.

When Gary finds himself not ahead of the others he's playing with, he may start grasping for ways to turn things around. Usually this involves taking risks that may put him in over his head. He will impulsively agree to a bet or a challenge even if he knows it may be beyond his skill set. He loses his focus, and any type of pre-shot routine he had goes out the window. He will recklessly try shots he's never made, be certain this is the time he can drive further than ever before, or confidently place money on his ability to pull off a shot that even a professional would find difficult. Today may be his day!

In order to avoid the consequences of this behavior, when Gary is aware of these behaviors kicking in, he should take advantage of these Mental Mulligans in order to avoid consequences:

- Focus
- Follow the Plan
- Step by step
- Be cautious, not careless
- Slow it down

YOLANDA — ANALYSIS PARALYSIS

When it comes to the game of golf, there aren't too many people as knowledgeable about its history, the rules, etiquette or even statistics about the course she is playing on than Yolanda. The discipline of the game is what appeals to Yolanda, and she takes her performance seriously.

When her game isn't going well, she starts to analyze every little aspect to try to figure out why she's playing poorly. As the round unfolds, if her performance doesn't improve, she can overanalyze each aspect of her game in an effort to figure out what's wrong so she can fix it. This can cause her to slow down the pace of play as she gets into the paralysis of analysis, analyzing every shot to try to identify the difference between good and poor performance. Even though others may suggest that she adapt to the conditions of the course or the people she's playing with, she will stay stuck in what's familiar and predictable for her.

When Yolanda starts to experience these behaviors, she would benefit from a Mental Mulligan from the list below:

- Lighten up
- Let go
- Take a chance
- Have some fun
- Flex

Each of the above scenarios describes real-life people who find their behavior changing into non-production actions that will limit their success, especially if there is a business deal at stake. You may find that you resonate with statements from multiple personas, and that is entirely reasonable.

The key point of this exercise is that you learn to recognize how you react when the pressure is on. What does your movement from strength to stress look like? When you've defined what this looks like, be prepared in advance by knowing which behaviors will offset the nonproductive reactions of stress. Learn ways to manage your behaviors so you can thrive in any set of circumstances and with any type of people, no matter how annoying they may be. They might hold the key to your next big deal!

ON COURSE WITH ... FLEMMING JORGENSEN
MANAGING DIRECTOR, COUNTRY LEADER SCANDINAVIA, DUPONT

Why I play golf: My mother was from California and we would spend summers visiting family up and down the West Coast. I was big into riding my bike and had sworn I would never play golf until maybe when I was retired. I was talked into playing a round in Sacramento at Valley Hi Country Club because a knee injury kept me off my bike. For my first round ever, at age 19, I shot a 102, having never held a club before. I was hooked. When I got back to Denmark, a friend and I signed up at a local club and played all the time. Within two years, my handicap was down to four.

How golf has helped me in business: I took an internship job at a chemical company when I was 21. My managing director wanted to learn how to play, so I took him with me. There's nothing like getting to spend a lot of time with your boss. After a stint in the Army, I came back to the company as a salesperson. I started hosting golf tournaments for customers, and 30 years later I'm still hosting them. In my role with DuPont, we hold an event every year and customers from all over Europe come to play. We give out great prizes and, for us, because of the products we make, a golf ball is like giving a sample of those products. Golf allows you to spend four to five hours with someone, which lets me to get to know the people I do business with very, very well. Everything relies on, "Are you the one who can deliver on time?" It's a partnership. You can't build these kinds of relationships with other sports, like tennis. You can't talk with people if they're on the other side of the net. And you have to be in shape to last in tennis. With golf, you can still play even if you're out of shape.

> " I've learned a lot of self-control. I can't blame others, the ball or the equipment for a bad shot. By looking inward, I learned how to find a way without making it other people's fault.
>
> — Flemming Jorgensen, Managing Director, Country Leader Scandinavia, DuPont "

How golf has made me more self-aware: When I was younger I learned early on how far I can throw a club. Since then, I've learned a lot of self-control. I can't blame others, the ball or the equipment for a bad shot. By looking inward, I learned how to find a way without making it other people's fault.

Relationships I've built through golf: About 24 years ago, I got a new customer in the polymer industry, and after a few visits we started to do business. He was the managing director/owner of a large Nordic cosmetics company, and we both found out we loved golf. We started to play a little golf together and see each other with our families on a private basis. As business grew, issues came along, like they do in the normal course of business, such as lack of delivery, pricing, claims, and we both found out that in order to keep our friendship, we had to give up the business relationship. He handed over the work to his purchasing manager, and I handed over my part of the work to the sales manager from my companies. Today his company has moved sales to the companies I have worked with, and we are still friends, traveling around the world playing golf, having family vacations, but no longer doing direct business between us. We still talk business on the golf course and on vacation, but it is more general market conditions and other business relations instead of direct orders. We are now members of the same club and play every week, and our companies are heading for 25 years of business together.

Advice for budding golfers: Make sure you try to become as good as you can. You get a lot more out of golf if you do. And you need a coach or a professional to help you learn. It's very much like leadership, where you need to take in views from those around you. Get a good start on the game with good equipment and good advice. That makes it fun.

10

HOW TO GET GOOD FAST

Jerry was a marketing executive with a major corporation in the technology sector that had long been involved with sports through a sponsorship of the America's Cup yacht race. The corporation provided both technical support for timing the races and promotional support as one of the title sponsors. Now it was wading into new waters (pardon the mixed metaphor) by becoming involved with one of the PGA Tour's official events.

When the corporation was sponsoring the America's Cup, it didn't have to get on a boat except to take a guided tour. But that was not so with the golf sponsorship. The company was required to participate in the Pro-Am. That's when Dave got the call. Here is his story:

The marketing executive explained with fear in his voice that he had been tasked with getting 12 what he called "bonafide nerds" up to speed and proficient at playing golf, something most of them had done only virtually — and he had to do it in a relatively short period of time.

Jerry and his team came to an intensive golf immersion program I was teaching. We worked on everything from developing some fundamental physical skills to a crash course in how to conduct themselves on the course: where to stand, when to hit, and how to gracefully take an X on a hole. It was an intensive five days, to be sure, but happily it all worked out. No one was hurt during the Pro-Am, at least not physically, and the company went on to stay involved with the tournament for years to come. Oh, and the original 12 "nerd" executives became avid "real" golfers.

The reason we share this story is because making the conscious decision to play business golf can be a voluntary one or it can be forced on you. In an earlier chapter we talked about whether or not skill matters, and depending on how you plan to use the game, it might. If, like Jerry, you are tossed into the deep end of the pool and expected to learn to swim FAST, then this chapter is for you.

You may not have the time or resources to go through a five-day program like Jerry's team, so what can you do to make rapid improvements to your golf game? We'll give you a variety of ways to chart a course for improving your game so you can reap the benefits. Here is some advice from Dave:

FIRST AND FOREMOST, FIND A COACH

You can save a lot of time and effort by going right to the source and finding someone who can give you individual coaching to improve specific areas where your performance is lacking.

Being a coach myself, one of the things I encounter with my students is they are overloaded with advice from well-meaning friends, televised tips, magazine articles and other sources. I'm not saying that all of this is bad … I'm just saying it's difficult to parse through it and discover what is relevant to *you*.

So when I say to find a coach, I mean find a PGA or LPGA professional who can customize an improvement plan for you. Finding someone who can assess your skills, understand your motivations, and outline a plan for achieving your goals can make all the difference in the world. You can check with your local club or course to find a professional, or another good resource is ***www.iMapGolf.com.***

TREAT YOURSELF TO A CUSTOM-FITTED SET OF GOLF CLUBS

There is an old saying that "A craftsman is only as good as his tools." That's true in work and in golf. I often hear people say "I'm not good enough for custom clubs" or "I'll wait until I'm good enough for custom clubs," and what I will then ask them is, "Did you wait until you were good at walking before you got shoes that fit?" It is one of the best investments you can make if you're serious about playing your best.

PRACTICE, PRACTICE, PRACTICE

Once you've taken care of these first two items, the next step is making the commitment to practice. We all have demands on our time. But the reality of developing your skills as a business golfer and lowering your handicap is it takes practice. The good news is it doesn't take a lot.

What follows is a system for organizing your practice time to get the most out of the time you have. The best place to start is to assess the current state of your game. The example below is what I ask my students to use. It breaks down the game into eight categories, which provides a baseline. The scores in the "PAR" section reveal the averages for a scratch handicap or par golfer. Your numbers will help you see which areas of your game need the most work.

SKILLS ASSESSMENT

COMPONENTS	PAR	YOUR AVERAGE	YOUR GOAL
FAIRWAYS HIT	65%		
TEE SHOT DISTANCE (YARDS)	242		
GREENS IN REGULATION	66%		
PITCH SHOTS % OF UP & DOWN	50%		
CHIP SHOTS % OF UP & DOWN	75%		
PUTTS PER ROUND	30		
SAND SAVES %	45%		
PENALTY SHOTS	.5%		

Source: Mental Edge™

Focus on the short game. Spending extra time on the shots that take place between the tee and the putting green is the best way to get better fast. Typically that's where we find the largest skill deficit. And since about 70 percent of all shots in a round of golf are within 80 yards of the green, focusing on your short game will pay dividends.

Don't fall into the distance trap. I have yet to meet any golfers who think they hit the ball too far. Nor have I seen a club company that promises less distance but more accuracy from its new driver. But distance is not everything. As you can see in the Skills Assessment, it doesn't take 300-yard drives to be a par golfer. Sure, it's fun to crank a long drive out there, but at the end of the day the drive that finds the fairway gives you the best chance to post a good score.

Be specific when you warm up. Virtually everyone who has played the game has encountered the Dr. Jekyll/Mr. Hyde experience when it comes to performance on the practice tee versus the golf course. On the range, you can flawlessly send ball after ball flying toward the target, and then you head out to the course and see your mastery evaporate. When this happens, golfers tend to react in one of two ways. Some avoid practice altogether. Since it doesn't seem to help their game, they say, "Why bother?" Others think, "If I just hit more balls, it will pay off on the course." Unfortunately, neither approach will work. Instead, your practice must support your specific performance goals on the course. Follow these cardinal rules for practice:

- **Think of practice as a warm-up and not a clinic.** Your warm-up should be 15 to 25 balls total, with five to 10 each of full and short swings. You are just loosening up. You've probably seen the following scenario: A golfer arrives at the course early and heads to the practice tee. During practice, the wheels fall off and the person panics and tries harder, which only makes matters worse. The golfer arrives at the first tee sweating, out of breath, and with a bad attitude. You know this individual will have a bad round. The reverse is also possible: The golfer goes to the range before tee time and hits fantastic shots and then heads to the tee full of confidence (and unrealistic expectations) for the round. So when the expectations aren't met, this individual's game unravels on the course.

- **Know when to stop.** When you warm up, quality is definitely more important than quantity. Don't feel compelled to "finish the pyramid" of golf balls sitting on the ground before you leave the range. Sure, it's hard to stop when you have just hit a perfect shot, but regardless of the reason, don't hit more than you need. Fatigue and loss of concentration are two indicators that a session is too long. To control fatigue, try not to hit more than 10 balls without a "mini-break." Take your hands off the club and collect your thoughts. Switch frequently between different clubs and shot techniques to keep your concentration fresh.

- **Don't neglect the trouble shots.** The purpose of practice is to avoid trouble on the golf course. However, on that odd occasion where you find yourself in a tough spot, the proper technique will allow you to escape with the least amount of damage to your score. Create trouble situations on the practice range such as shots out of the rough or off the hard pan. Uneven lies and fairway bunker shots are other examples.

WHY PRACTICE?

Before you begin your practice session, try to determine what you want to accomplish. Be specific as to why you practice. This is a prime element in your ability to "self-coach" as you improve your game. There are four major reasons to practice:
- Curative: To address and attempt to cure a specific problem.
- Developmental: To integrate new techniques.
- Maintenance: To maintain your current skill level.
- Strategic: To modify your technique to fit certain conditions, such as wind or rain.

WHAT TO PRACTICE

After you identify "why to practice," move on to "what to practice." Focus your session on the parts of your game where your performance does not meet your goals. For instance, if your chip shot percentage is under your goal, then allocate practice time for accuracy. What would it do to your scores if you could improve your chip shot percentage by 20 percent?

There are a number of different ways to practice, and as is the case in almost any endeavor, you get out what you put in. Remember, you decide to practice on the premise that it will improve your performance and enjoyment under playing conditions. It may sound like practice isn't fun, but that doesn't have to be the case! Go out and hit balls just for the fun of it. Be careful not to get judgmental or upset if you hit a bad one. After all, when there isn't a specific objective for a session, anything could happen. Most of the time you should try to keep your practice sessions performance-related and focused on your goal.

While it isn't necessary to be proficient at the game to be able to take advantage of the opportunities it affords, I can tell you that Jerry and his team cemented long-lasting and beneficial relationships because they took their games to school. As their golf handicap improved, their "Business Golf Handicap" also improved. Coincidence? I don't think so.

ON COURSE WITH ... BOB McCOY
CONSULTANT AND FORMER WALL STREET ANALYST,
GOLF ADVENTURER, HTTP://THEGOLFODYSSEY.COM

Between 1973 and 1988, I worked as a sell-side equity analyst for Kidder Peabody in New York City. Part of the job was to travel to every major city in the United States twice a year and overseas every 18 months to talk to clients who were money managers. In the early 1970s *Golf Digest* published a list of the top 100 courses in the USA. Then in 1979 *Golf Magazine* came out with a list of the top 50 courses in the world, which was expanded to the top 100 in 1985.

I got the urge to play all courses on both lists. So when I planned a sales trip, I would suggest to the salesman in Los Angeles, or Chicago, or Atlanta that he ask a couple of clients to play Los Angeles Country Club, or Chicago Golf Club, or Atlantic Country Club. Not only was this a way to get on many highly rated private courses, but Kidder paid for the transportation and greens fee. Everyone was happy: The salesman was entertaining clients, the clients were playing a very good course, and I was checking off another course on the list as well as getting to know clients on an informal basis.

Our London office introduced me to true links golf in the UK and Ireland beginning in 1979. One time I did a round-the-world business trip to play in Japan, Indonesia and South Africa. Thanks to Kidder, I became the first person in the world to play the top 100 courses in the USA (1984) and the top 100 in the world (1988). I also became a golf course rater. Every two years, between five and 10 courses are added to and subtracted from each list, and I have stayed current with all the changes over the years.

11

RULES OF THE GAME

Everyone knows golf is a game of many rules. But there is one golden rule for the game as it applies to business: Golf unto them as they would golf unto themselves.

In other words, try to make this five-hour relationship-building opportunity as comfortable as possible. Your success will come in direct relation to the pre-golf information you can gather about your client's golfing abilities, personality and preferences.

If the client has accepted your invitation to play, you're the host; if the client invited you, some other business golf customs are in play. Either way, the more you know of the client's golf background, the better prepared you'll be to understand what rules govern the day. For instance, an accomplished golfer will likely want to stick to the published rules of the game. A beginner may be intimidated by them.

There is only one set of official rules, and you might even run into a traditionalist who insists they be applied even to your casual game. When that's the case, a safe solution may be to plead rule confusion and ask the traditionalist to act as sort of a rules coach as the round progresses. Your flattery will likely enhance the experience.

KEY RULES EVERYONE SHOULD KNOW

Some of the entries in the current 206-page *Rules of Golf* published by the United States Golf Association are especially important to know in any situation. Knowing these will show you have a respect for the official rules, if not a thorough knowledge:

Rule #10: Order of play. Know who plays first — and in what order — on the tee box, on the fairway and after you reach the green.

Rule #13: The ball must be played as it lies. Learn the exceptions — such as when you get relief from obstructions and when you do not.

Rule #16: The putting green. Know how to mark your ball, whether you can clear your putting path, and related rules when you're on the green.

Rule #26: Water hazards. If you hit your ball into a water hazard, know where to drop a new ball and hit another shot.

Rule #27: Lost ball, or a ball hit out of bounds. Both incur "stroke and distance" penalties. Know how to declare and hit a provisional ball, commonly known as "three from the tee."

Generally, though, most games that do not involve an agreed-upon competition will waive some of golf's onerous rules and get on with having a fun day hitting a ball on the ground with a stick over grass somebody else had to mow.

WHEN TO BEND THE RULES

Golf rules evolve, and so should your application of them in a business relationship golf day. One of the best ways is to have an open-ended conversation about it before you tee off. Some of the rules that might get "informally bent" in a business golf environment are:

- **Play the ball as it lies.** Preferred lies, where you can adjust a ball's position in fairways, is a common bend.
- **After five minutes of searching, the ball is deemed lost.** For the sake of speed of play, this length of time is often informally truncated.
- **Relief cannot be obtained from conditions such as a footprint in a bunker.** Frequently this is waived during informal play.

RULES INVOLVING HAZARDS

One way to display your golfing savvy is to know and practice the rules that govern situations when your ball goes into a hazard. Most hazards involve bodies of water, such as ponds, lakes and rivers. But sometimes they can be other special conditions, such as environmentally protected areas.

There are two types of golf hazards as they pertain to the rules. The boundary of a hazard is defined by yellow stakes and/or lines on the ground. The boundary of a lateral hazard is defined by red stakes and/or lines on the ground.

If a ball enters a hazard marked in yellow, a player has the following options:

1. Play the ball as it lies without grounding the club prior to hitting a shot. (No penalty)
2. Drop the ball behind the hazard on a line extending from the hold through the point where the ball last crossed the hazard margin. (One-stroke penalty)
3. Drop the ball at the point of the last shot. (One-stroke penalty)

If a ball enters a lateral hazard marked in red, a player has the above options plus two more:

4. Drop the ball within two club lengths of the point where the ball last entered the hazard, no nearer the hold.
5. Drop the ball within two club lengths of a point on the opposite margin of the hazard that is equidistant from the hole from where the ball last crossed the margin of the lateral hazard (a creek for example), but no closer to the hole.

A couple of other hazard tidbits:

- The stakes defining a hazard may be removed if they obstruct a player's shot.
- A local rule may provide a drop zone near a hazard as an additional place for a player to drop the ball for the next shot.

Sometimes there are conditions that allow for "no penalty" relief from objects on the golf course such as cart paths, sprinkler heads or a drainage ditch. Often they are printed on scorecards if unusual. One key to remember in the "free relief situations" is they usually give one club length relief rather than the two club lengths you use when you pay a stroke penalty.

If you are an avid golfer, adopt a beginner or two. They'll be grateful, and you'll be advancing the sport. If you're a beginner, relax because golfers are givers, and most of them love to share. The rules will become clear to you eventually. In the meantime, remember to enjoy yourself.

WARTIME RULES OF GOLF

Golf is an evolving sport, and even the most rigid rules-followers have to be flexible in some situations. Consider these variations on the rules of golf from the World War II era in Great Britain.

 1. PLAYERS ARE ASKED TO COLLECT BOMB AND SHRAPNEL SPLINTERS TO SAVE THESE CAUSING DAMAGE TO THE MOWING MACHINES.

2. IN COMPETITIONS, DURING GUNFIRE, OR WHILE BOMBS ARE FALLING, PLAYERS MAY TAKE COVER WITHOUT PENALTY FOR CEASING PLAY.

3. THE POSITIONS OF KNOWN DELAYED-ACTION BOMBS ARE MARKED BY RED FLAGS PLACED AT REASONABLY, BUT NOT GUARANTEED SAFE DISTANCE THEREFROM.

4. SHRAPNEL AND/OR BOMB SPLINTERS ON THE FAIRWAYS, OR IN BUNKERS WITHIN A CLUB'S LENGTH OF A BALL MAY BE MOVED WITHOUT PENALTY, AND NO PENALTY SHALL BE INCURRED IF A BALL IS THEREBY CAUSED TO MOVE ACCIDENTALLY.

5. A BALL MOVED BY ENEMY ACTION MAY BE REPLACED, OR IF LOST OR DESTROYED, A BALL MAY BE DROPPED NOT NEARER THE HOLE WITHOUT PENALTY.

6. A BALL LYING IN A CRATER MAY BE LIFTED AND DROPPED NOT NEARER THE HOLE, PRESERVING THE LINE TO THE HOLE WITHOUT PENALTY.

7. A PLAYER WHOSE STROKE IS AFFECTED BY THE SIMULTANEOUS EXPLOSION OF A BOMB MAY PLAY ANOTHER BALL FROM THE SAME PLACE. PENALTY, ONE STROKE.

ON COURSE WITH ... DAN ALLEN
CHAIRMAN AND CEO, SERCO

Why I play golf: I didn't get started playing golf until I was in my early 30s. I was talking with my boss one day about what my next career steps should be and was contemplating getting an MBA. I had gone to him for advice about which program I should consider, and I was totally surprised by his response. He said, "If you want to be a leader, forget an MBA and learn how to play golf." And I did. It turned out to be some of the best advice I've been given. Golf gives you a platform for how you can grow in your career.

How golf has helped me in business: I have built many alliances and relationships on the golf course. Because I invested in getting good at the game, I always got to play with the better golfers. When I was with GTE, the entire executive team played golf. I got to take a team out every week. When we were bought by General Dynamics, that golf culture allowed me to quickly build a network, and I learned who the good guys were and weren't. Because of my skill, when we hosted a corporate outing at the Phoenician in Phoenix I was paired with the CEO of one of our major clients simply because I was the best golfer. The relationships and exposure through golf I got early in my career opened up opportunities for me.

> *Golf provides a great means to understand the people you work with. It allows you to build relationships with your customers and enables awareness of what they need.*
>
> — Dan Allen,
> Chairman and CEO, Serco

I remember a time when General Dynamics sponsored a senior PGA event. It was between 2001 and 2002, and the Internet wasn't part of the infrastructure. We had built a network integration business and we needed partners. Cisco was an obvious choice, but they were treating us as one of many. We invited the CEO from Cisco to come play in the Pro Am. Because of this, we were able to demonstrate how we could be a better partner with Cisco.

How golf has made me more self-aware: My son Zach lived with his Mom, so it was difficult to get to spend quality time with him. Although he had never played golf, I was able to get him out on the course with me. It gave us a way to have a stronger relationship because of the time we were able to spend together. As a parent, I was able to use golf as a forum to focus on the things I wanted him to learn. Now, I'm proud to say, Zach is a golf professional.

How golf has helped me develop business relationships: In my business, if people make an ethical mistake, it becomes public knowledge. I need to trust who I work with, and playing golf gives me that insight. Golf gives a way to see the intangibles in people. The two most important ones are the ability to follow rules and the ability to demonstrate respect. Golf is all about rules and yet there is no referee to enforce them. When I work with people, I need to know that they will follow the rules. Otherwise, I'm going to have to create a culture of compliance, which requires a lot of supervision. With regard to respect, at the end of the round, no matter who won or how you played, we shake each other's hand. I look for people to partner with who can follow the rules and demonstrate respect for their competitor.

Advice for novice golfers: Golf provides a great means to understand the people you work with. It allows you to build relationships with your customers and enables awareness of what they need. Go play golf with your team members. Play with the people on the shop floor. It's a tool to interact personally and with your teams.

12

ETIQUETTE OF THE GAME

Golf has its own unique customs and rules of etiquette. These act as traffic signals, helping the flow of the game. To carry on the traffic metaphor, it doesn't matter whether you're steering a truck, a sedan or a bike, these rules all pretty much apply to make every golf experience better. They ensure a smooth ride so golf's orderly and pastoral landscape can unfold and allow for bonding and friendship building.

Whether you're a skilled golfer, a beginner or somewhere in between, your knowledge and practice of golf's time-honored traditions will forever make a favorable impression on your playing partners. In business golf, this will reflect more positively on you than any other effort you can make. Conversely, a glaring golf faux pas can indelibly affect the key relationship golf could bring you with a client.

Golf etiquette and customs aren't limited to the green grasses of the golfing grounds. They begin and continue before and after the round.

Depending on where your business golf game is going to be played, there may be customs and rules of etiquette that are unique to that venue. Before you arrive, it's wise to invest in a call to the professional staff. You can do this anonymously so they aren't aware that you're not already in the know.

ESSENTIAL ETIQUETTE RULES FOR BUSINESS GOLF

RESPECT THE SPIRIT OF THE GAME. GOLF IS SELF-SUPERVISED. IT RELIES ON YOUR PERSONAL INTEGRITY TO PLAY BY THE RULES, AND TO BE CONSIDERATE OF OTHER PLAYERS.

PRACTICE "SAFETY FIRST." KNOW WHERE OTHERS ARE WHEN YOU MAKE A PRACTICE SWING OR HIT A SHOT. NEVER HIT INTO THE GROUP AHEAD OF YOU. YELL "FORE!" IF YOUR BALL MAY HIT SOMEONE.

SLOW PLAY IS A MORTAL SIN! KEEP UP WITH THE GROUP AHEAD OF YOU. BE READY TO HIT WHEN IT IS YOUR TURN TO PLAY. IF YOU ARE HOLDING UP THE GROUP BEHIND YOU, WAVE THEM TO PLAY THROUGH.

RESPECT THE COURSE. REPAIR BALL MARKS ON THE GREEN, EVEN IF THEY ARE NOT YOURS. REPLACE DIVOTS YOU MAKE ON THE TEE BOX OR FAIRWAY. RAKE BUNKERS AS YOU LEAVE THEM. DON'T DRIVE GOLF CARTS OR TROLLEYS CLOSE TO A GREEN, OR STEP ON THE CUP.

RESPECT YOUR FELLOW GOLFERS. STAND OUT OF ANOTHER PLAYER'S SIGHT LINE. AVOID STEPPING ON ANOTHER PLAYER'S PUTTING LINE ON THE GREEN. DON'T OFFER UNSOLICITED ADVICE. ALWAYS COMPLIMENT A GOOD SHOT!

Some of the insider information you should seek includes:

- Are cell phones allowed or prohibited on the grounds?
- What is the dress code?
- Are caddies mandatory?
- Are golf cars required?
- Are lockers and showers available?
- Are spikeless golf shoes required? (Today they are almost universally used.)
- Can you pitch and chip to the practice putting green?

Often, there are more, so be sure to ask whether there's anything special you ought to know before showing up to meet your playing partner. Today a lot of business golf occurs at more expensive public golf courses that aspire to provide a "country club" service experience. If you intend to use that type of venue as the site of your business golf activity, you should visit there well in advance. This will allow the staff to put your face and name together so that when you do arrive with your client, you'll be given a respectful level of service. As an insurance policy, find ways to offer healthy advance gratuities to the greeters and professional staff. It is the way of the world. Golf staffs have elephant-like memory.

So, on to the golf course. Previously we discussed business golf's golden rule, and this is where it should be applied with sensitivity. For those of you who are experienced golfers, let the following be a review. For you who are new, showing respect and practicing these customs and rules of etiquette will brand you as a decent golf partner.

RULES ON THE COURSE

- Be on time! Tee times are perishable inventory.
- When you injure the course, fix it. Replace divots made in the fairway and sometimes even in the rough. When you have to play from a sand bunker, enter from its lowest point and then be sure the surface is raked to playable conditions for those who follow. When your ball dents the putting surface, repair it. If you see a scar someone else failed to repair, fix that, too.

- Avoid walking across another player's intended line of play as that individual prepares. This applies everywhere, but on the putting green be especially careful not to step on the intended line of a putt because causing a foot impression could divert the pure roll of the ball.
- First in gets the pin. That is, whoever finishes putting first is charged with picking up the flagstick and returning it when play on that hole is complete.
- When asked to "tend the pin" while another putts, be sure to hold the flag in such a way that it does not flutter in the wind.
- Carry a small wet towel and clean your golf ball when the rules allow you to touch it — on the tee and on the green.
- Be prepared to play. This applies especially if you are playing in a golf cart and you can safely walk to your ball while your playing partner is preparing to play. Guesstimate the club you might need and take the one you think you need and one longer and one shorter with you. If the grass is wet, bring another towel and put the unused clubs on it so the grips don't get slippery.
- If you're driving the golf cart, respect the daily posted use. That can include using paths only or 90-degree crossing of fairways. As a general rule, keep the golf cart at least 50 feet away from putting greens. Before putting, park the cart between the green and the next tee box.
- Record your score at the next tee, not before you leave the previous green area. This allows the people behind you to get to the greens more quickly, which speeds up play on the whole course.
- In casual play, a process called "ready golf" is usually if effect. That is, the first player deemed ready to play can do just that, in the spirit of continuing a smooth pace of play. Ready golf on the tee is easy. On the fairway, safety issues come into play and you and your playing partners should use your best judgment to decide who hits first.

Before we move along, we should talk about the last big golf custom that new golfers need explained. It has to do with noise on the golf course. To outsiders, it might look silly.

In other sports, fans are screaming, cowbells are clanging and feet are stomping while the athletes are performing perfectly and it doesn't bother them. In many cases the noise actually motivates them to better performance.

The foul shot in basketball is a perfect example. But in golf, noise distracts and destroys concentration and ultimately good golf swings ... and a lot of people don't understand why.

It's the predictability factor. That foul-shooting basketball player fully expects pompoms to be waving and feet to be stomping while he sends the ball toward the hoop. That player would be just as equally distracted if the crowd were quiet and an unexpected air horn blast rang out just at the instant he released the ball.

So on the golf course, where nature's tranquil ways are a big part of the culture, unexpected sound is a big distraction. Birds chirp. Winds whistle. Brooks babble. That's expected and isn't a bother. But when people babble unexpectedly, that is a distraction to many golfers, and it's why the etiquette of the game is stringent about unpredictable noise. If you can avoid making it while others are attending to their golf shot, you will make many friends.

What kinds of noise? That's a good one! Clinking clubs together. Cell phones. Squeaky golf cart brakes. The ripping sound of golf glove Velcro. Chit-chat. Food wrappers. Bouncing balls. Squirting aerosols. Footsteps. The key is awareness. Noise travels — especially over water, where you can wind up distracting players on other holes, too.

Your sounds might be inevitable. When you have to sneeze, you have to sneeze. But realize you might have to be contrite afterward if the noise contributes to a lack of concentration for any of your golfing partners. Making an effort to manage the timing of sounds builds golfing respect. The distraction factor is all about when and whether or not the sound was expected.

The same can apply for sudden movements, so try and stand where you are out of the fringe vision of other players while they're making a shot. We knew one scurrilous gambler who used the sun as a co-conspirator. He'd use his shadow to distract and even went so far as to polish his putter to a mirror-like sheen and would flash it in his opponent's face at critical times. Needless to say, his tactics hastened his shunning.

Just as in hopscotch, flag football, and dancing there are certain behaviors unique to each culture that may not make sense to a casual observer but are honored by those who choose to entertain themselves that way. People who want to play golf figure out early on that the customs, manners and rules are part of its charm.

And golf is constantly evolving. Rules change. Customs change. Once you're a golfer, being aware of those changes is part of the attraction.

If your clients are golfers, your knowledge of the game's unwritten rules, etiquette and customs will cement their respect for you on the green grass and very likely in their place of business.

- -

 ## THE 19ᵀᴴ HOLE

THERE ARE ETIQUETTE RULES FOR THE 19TH HOLE, TOO. WHEN YOU GET OFF THE COURSE AND INTO THE CLUBHOUSE, HERE ARE SOME THINGS TO KEEP IN MIND:

RELAX AND TALK ABOUT THE GAME: YOUR PARTNER'S GOOD SHOTS, GOOD HOLES, HOW ENJOYABLE THE GAME WAS. (IF BETS WERE MADE, SETTLE UP. IF YOU WON, PAY FOR THE DRINKS.)

NOW IT'S OK TO TALK SOME BUSINESS. BRIEFLY. FOLLOW UP ON ANY BUSINESS TOPIC MENTIONED EARLIER. BRING UP A TOPIC YOU'D LIKE TO DISCUSS. IF MORE TIME IS NEEDED, ARRANGE AN OFFICE APPOINTMENT.

LET'S DO THIS AGAIN. INVITE YOUR GUEST TO PLAY GOLF AGAIN, OR TAKE A LESSON TOGETHER, OR ATTEND A GOLF EVENT. ASK YOUR CLIENT TO SUGGEST OTHERS WHO MIGHT JOIN YOU NEXT TIME.

- -

ON COURSE WITH ... JIM TRAINHAM
CHIEF TECHNOLOGY OFFICER, JDC PHOSPHATE INC.

Why I play golf: I started caddying for my aunt when I was nine years old. I fell in love with the game watching her play. I was also a fan of Arnold Palmer and still have his Shot Maker clubs that I bought with my paper route money. My father thought it was too expensive, but I played despite that fact. I had a single-digit handicap by the time I was 17 but stopped playing because I tore up my knee.

How golf has helped me in business: I've traveled the globe on business, and being able to play golf has allowed me to get to know people — especially in Asia, where they like to entertain you and are always looking for an excuse to play. Because I like to play, I would always go somewhere early and play with my managers, which helped me build relationships with them and allowed me to play some great courses around the world. I was able to interact at a high level with people in other companies.

> *If you're going to be good, you have to be dedicated, especially to play with customers. It takes work. If you're going to play as part of your professional portfolio, you have to play to a handicap below 20.*
>
> — Jim Trainham,
> Chief Technology Officer,
> JDC Phosphate Inc.

How golf has made me more self-aware: There are two different kinds of golf: fun and competitive — and they are very different. Competitive golf teaches you to control your emotions so your body responds the way you want it to. In business, if you can be cooler under pressure and know how your body responds and how to relax, you can get your emotions under control. The adrenalin is channeled. When I was with PPG Industries, I was playing at the Buick Pro-Am. There were 1,000 people lining the fairway, and Tiger Woods had just teed off before me. I had never played the course and had to ask the caddy where the hole was. The best shot was over the crowd, but the risk was that you'd kill somebody. The adrenalin was pumping, but I hit a dead-perfect shot. That kind of pressure teaches you how to channel the anxiety. I've never felt as nervous as that shot, which makes business pressure easier to deal with.

Advice for the golf novice: If you're going to be good, you have to be dedicated, especially to play with customers. It takes work. If you're going to play as part of your professional portfolio, you have to play to a handicap below 20. Golf is totally addictive. If you love it, you're sunk.

13

WHAT IF YOU'RE PLAYING WITH A ROOKIE?

W e've talked about how you and your guests will come to the game with a variety of experience levels. So what happens when your guest is a complete novice? This scenario presents both an opportunity and a potential for disaster. Dave explains it this way:

My wife is a former ski instructor and has many stories of rescuing skiers who had ventured onto terrain that was far beyond their skill set to traverse. It can be terrifying for the individual as well as embarrassing for certain egos to have to be led down the mountain to safer terrain.

My point with this story is that most of the time the people who put their fellow skier in such an awkward position had the best of intentions. Although misguided, the intent was usually to share a fun activity together. However, if everyone isn't of the same skill level, the activity can result in a disaster, both physically and emotionally.

In skiing, beginners belong on the "bunny slopes" learning basic skills and then progressing to steeper, more challenging runs as their skills improve. In the game of golf, there unfortunately isn't a "bunny slope." So how do you handle it when faced with the prospect of playing with a beginner or a relative newcomer to the game?

BUILD CONFIDENCE

The very best way to ensure a successful experience with a rookie golfer is to control the environment. We suggest you share a lesson or two as a way of introducing novices to the game, helping them get a grasp of the fundamentals. Offer to meet them for practice sessions to monitor progress, along with follow-up lessons to help them gain confidence to eventually get out and play. Shepherd them along so when they do go on the course they are prepared and don't feel like that skier stuck on the side of the mountain.

Now that describes the best-case scenario, where you have the opportunity to control the process. We have seen this played out a number of times with great success. The relationships that are built because an enlightened *Back On Course* golfer took the time to help someone develop skills can pay dividends well into the future.

Here's another scenario that is more complicated. You participate in your company-sponsored scramble event, and as you introduce yourself to your teammates, "Joe" lets you know this is his first time ever on a golf course … and he has heard that you're really good and is looking forward to getting lot of pointers from you.

We can feel some of you gripping the book a little tighter. Maybe you've had this experience? It can make for a long day and, if managed poorly, leave a bad impression on a current or potential client. This will test your situational management skills for sure, so here is some advice.

Before you head to the practice tee, check with the pro shop to see if they have a professional who can do a quick, what we call a "Just-in-time," coaching session to give the novice a basic grip-alignment-posture clinic with some rudimentary swing motion tips.

ASSIGN A ROLE

If there isn't a professional available, the next best thing is to head to the putting green. Since a beginning golfer has trouble getting the ball in the air, you can focus on the part of the game that doesn't require that skill.

Start rookies close to the hole — no more than a foot — and have them putt it in the cup. You can move them back from the hole a foot at time to give them some sense of distance and directional control. You can show them the basics of greens reading and demonstrate how slopes affect the direction. You can tell them that the rest of the group will take care of the long shots and they can focus on the putts.

It's amazing how this takes the pressure off of them and how often they will actually make a putt that contributes to the team. Beyond that, your job for the day is to stay patient, give encouragement, hunt for a few golf balls … and make sure you are in control of the pairings for your next company event.

A LASTING IMPRESSION

As we said in the opening statement for this chapter, playing with a rookie represents an amazing opportunity. You just need to be able to capitalize on it.

We've heard countless stories where an experience with golf early on in a person's life had a tremendous impact on his or her future in the game. Some were positive and influenced a person to take it up as a lifelong pursuit, which allowed them to reap the benefits of the relationships made. Doors opened because of that little white ball.

We have also heard horror stories of experiences that were personally embarrassing or made people feel left out because they didn't play. If you are a golfer, welcome a rookie into the game. If you are a rookie, seek out opportunities to take up the game.

ON COURSE WITH ... ELIZABETH SHELLEY
SENIOR VICE PRESIDENT,
MANAGER COMMERCIAL HEALTHCARE LENDING, WEBSTER BANK

A couple years back, I was participating in a company-sponsored client golf outing. My foursome included a senior credit officer, two clients and me. As a lead-up to the event, I heard that one of my clients was working on his game going into the weekend to be ready for Monday. On Sunday I received a text message from him saying his game was awful and he really didn't want to embarrass himself by playing in the event. I texted him back not to worry about it, to just be sure he was at the event the next day.

As many company outings go, there was a format to this one, and one of my clients failed to show, so we were a threesome playing with format rules. One of the first things out of my client's mouth was "Ugh." I told him we were there to get to know each other and to have fun. If that meant we didn't compete for the prize, as long as we kept our pace of play we'd be fine. I encouraged my team to play our own scramble.

> "He uses me as a financial advisor now as well as his commerical banker.
>
> — Elizabeth Shelley, Senior Vice President, Manager Commerical Healthcare Lending, Webster Bank"

It was an excellent idea based on our talent pool, and it also allowed the customer to relax. I did my best to keep it in the fairway so the rest of the team had a shot we could use. He figured out that I wasn't confined by boxes just because there were boxes, but that I wasn't a total "cowboy" about it. This has stood me well for this client, who realizes that I'm not just a "cookie cutter" banker but someone who can think on my feet. He uses me as a financial advisor now as well as his commercial banker.

He told me he was glad he showed up that day.

14

THE FORWARD TEES:
FOR WOMEN ONLY

I t's exciting to watch women golf professionals play. Many of them have
spent time on golf courses since they were young girls. But the truth is
that most women in business are not used to being on the golf course...
yet. They are in the minority in a sport that men have embraced for much
longer. So there are things women should know about how to approach the
sport, what is appropriate in a round of business golf, and the special rules
of etiquette that apply only to women. Here is Connie's take on it:

My first real experience playing corporate golf was when I was working for DuPont and the company held a team event at a resort in Tarpon
Springs, Florida. I was facilitating some workshops for the event, and someone else organized a golf tournament.

I had the time of my life — partly because everyone, except for the
person who put together the event, was a really bad golfer. One person even
wore cowboy boots because that's all he had brought with him and he was
told it was a mandatory team-building event. But he showed up, along with
everyone else, and the group had a blast.

Looking back on that experience, I see how unique it was and how
fortunate I was that I didn't get scared off by a bunch of intimidating male
golfers with low handicaps. In the work world, you are often very conscious
of the causes for intimidation. But on the golf course, you sometimes don't
even know what you don't know. The business golf rules you're playing by
on any given day can be unspoken until you learn to clarify them.

And it's hard going back to being a "rookie" when you're used to being
seen as a competent, successful businesswoman. But it's an insider's game,
and women are often on the outside. I learned that the day I walked into the
men's club at a private course. I didn't even know such a thing existed.

This chapter is not to whine and complain about how poorly the game of golf has treated women. The rules have changed in the last several years, and women are more accepted on the course today. Some long-term glass ceilings have been shattered. That's behind us, and it's time to move on.

Instead, I hope to offer some practical suggestions that will help women pick up a set of clubs and get out there to play more corporate golf. If you choose to skip the golf portion of a business outing, you're missing out on business opportunities you won't get while you're sitting by the pool. Business is all about relationships, and there is no better way to cement a friendship than spending a day at the golf course.

YOU ARE NOT ALONE

One big myth is that you have to be good to play golf with anyone, but especially with men. That is just not true. I once stayed in a hotel in Ann Arbor, Michigan, that overlooked a golf course. I was on a high floor, which gave me a view of about half the course. I was really surprised to watch the action and see all of the missed shots and lost balls. I was relieved I was not the only one struggling to straighten out my tee shot. It gave me hope.

A friend of mine who was an executive with a pharmaceutical company called me one day and said, "I have to play in this event and I've never even held a club. It's next week. What do I do?" I spent an afternoon at a par 3 executive course with her and we focused on some simple basics: Don't drive the cart on the greens. Know why the clubs are called woods and irons, and how some woods aren't even made of wood.

While she was really not transformed into a great golfer in a week, my friend did get the courage to show up to her event. She was the only woman there. At the awards banquet for the event, the organizers presented her with a special trophy, and everyone stood and applauded her for being a good sport. The business value was immense, even if she didn't hit a tee shot more than 50 yards.

If you are a new golfer and your skills are limited, you can still play with the pros. There are several things to keep in mind if you're in that situation:

- Don't be afraid to play from the forward tees or "ladies tees." Even though it might feel as if you're taking an advantage based on gender, it will give you some hope of keeping up with the men in your group.

The forward tees were designed to compensate for the differences in upper body strength between men and women, so leverage them. And be prepared when it's your turn to hit your tee shot so you don't slow down the pace of the game.

- Tell the others in your foursome that you're new to the game and that you will stay conscious of the pace of play. If all of you are playing your own ball, tell them you'll pick yours up if it's a bad shot so you won't hold them up.

- Be especially attentive about golf etiquette because this will matter more than your own performance. Revisit *Chapter 12: Etiquette of the Game* if necessary.

- Be a cheerleader for the foursome. Compliment people on great shots. Keep the conversation light and lively so everyone finds it enjoyable to have you in the group. This will take the attention off of your game.

- Buy your playing partners a round of drinks or snacks when the beverage cart comes around, and remember to tip the attendant. That shows you know what you're doing.

- Look the part. Make sure you're wearing appropriate golf attire and have the extras like ball markers or a towel for wiping your clubs. Even a ball retriever for fetching a golf ball out of low water may prove to be useful at some point.

- Ask for advice — not on every shot, but where it makes sense. When the shot looks like it could be tricky for you, ask "Anyone have any advice? I really don't know how to play this." Sometimes all you may need is a simple adjustment that could make a difference.

In summary, if you're new to the game of golf, don't let that stop you from participating. The two most important things to remember are: Don't slow down the game, and have a good time.

PUT YOURSELF OUT THERE

As a woman, you need to remember that often it doesn't occur to your male colleagues to invite you to participate. Because there has been so little participation in corporate golf events by women, your lack of an invitation may indeed be accidental. So speak up. Ask to be included.

If you are a fairly good golfer and a woman, you are a real asset to a foursome, especially if the event is a scramble where you're playing "best ball." A good female golfer playing from forward tees brings a distinct advantage to her foursome where the other three are males and may be required to play from a greater distance. Many men have figured this out and recruit women to be on their teams so they can benefit from that advantage.

There are other ways women can use golf as a business advantage even while not on the course. Make sure you're up to speed on the televised tournaments and that you know the players so you can carry on an intelligent conversation before or after meetings. Know about resorts or great courses to play. Subscribe to a golf magazine so you're up on the latest and greatest equipment and apparel. Many airline clubs and in-flight magazines cater to golfers, so you can always increase your golf knowledge that way.

A great way for women to build up their confidence on the golf course is to play with other women. There are many great businesswomen golfers who are more than happy to help other women get started. Look for after-work leagues at a local golf course, or your company may even sponsor one. There are also conferences for women that offer golf instruction or a tournament that can be a great way to build up your confidence.

Take some lessons, but not from just anyone. Get someone who plays well to refer you to a good golf instructor. It does not necessarily need to be a woman coach, but it should be someone who has worked with women who are serious about the game.

Invest in some clubs that fit you and your swing. They don't need to be custom-fitted, but they should not be your husband/boyfriend/father's castaways. If you're new to the game, you don't even need to get a driver right away but can get by with a 3-wood for your drives. A 5 iron and a putter will be the other two clubs most used.

Sometimes it's hard for women to play corporate golf because they just don't like the game. Think of it as an investment in your career rather than a recreational activity. Find out what aspect of the game really does appeal to you and focus on that. Do you enjoy it most when you're playing with friends? If so, get an agreement to play with them on a consistent basis. You'll see your game improve immensely because of the consistency. Is it just being outside playing on a beautiful course, enjoying the sunshine and an opportunity to relax, that makes for a great round of golf for you? If so, don't play during peak hours, and try to go to different courses rather than the same one. Is it hitting the ball far that lights your fire? Then go to the practice range and spend 20 to 30 minutes each time hitting a bucket of balls. If learning something new is important to you, then set some performance goals and track your progress.

These are some simple ways to find pleasure in the game even if you know you're doing it as a business strategy. Maybe you'll be surprised to find that someday you really develop a love for golf.

ON COURSE WITH ... CECE DECAMP
VICE PRESIDENT, INTEGRATION EXECUTIVE, IBM GLOBAL SERVICES

Why I play golf: I play for fun and for business. I choose golf for fun because I like that I can sometimes play by myself, sometimes with a group I know, sometimes competitively, and mostly because I like being outdoors. The very first time I played golf was at an outing at work. In the late 1980s, I was young and athletic and one of my male coworkers asked, "Can you hit a golf ball?" I thought, well I can hit a softball, so why not? Of course, what was happening was the annual golf outing was a scramble and they wanted someone who could hit from the front tees to get the guys a little closer on the Par 5s. I filled my end of that bargain and more as I went out and practiced ahead of the day and showed up with just enough knowledge of what I was to do, an understanding of golf etiquette, and just enough of a golf game to get invited out again to play rounds with the guys even when it wasn't a scramble. It didn't hurt that I had caught the golf bug — and big time! I was out playing every weekend after that, wanting to get better and go out on tour at any moment. Well, I didn't make the tour, but I did get good enough that I was comfortable playing in almost any environment.

> "
> *You don't practice and play enough to get that mad at your game.*
>
> — CeCe DeCamp,
> Vice President,
> Integration Executive,
> IBM Global Services
> "

How golf has helped me in business: I work with federal government clients, and you can't offer them gifts or items of value such as a paid-for golf round. But I learned that most of my senior C-suite government clients were passionate about one charity or another. So whenever there was a charity fundraising golf event, I was quick to join in. Nearly every year, my company pays for a sponsorship or a foursome at a golf tournament for the Border Patrol Foundation, which honors the memory of U.S. Border Patrol agents, helps those injured in the line of duty, and supports their families. At one of these events I was able to meet senior members of the Border Patrol and develop relationships that proved very helpful when it was time to go visit them in their offices.

A really cool golf experience: Through my company, I was able to take a business colleague as my guest to the U.S. Open golf tournament at the prestigious Oakmont Country Club in Pennsylvania, which has hosted more USGA and PGA championships than any other course in America. It was a lot of fun spending time watching great golf, hanging out having food and drinks in our tent along the 18th fairway, and networking. A few months later, the colleague asked, "Would you like to play Oakmont?" WOW! That is like asking your seven-year-old if she wants to see Mickey Mouse — heck yeah! My colleague had attended a charity event and won a silent auction item of three rounds of golf to be played with an Oakmont member. I got to be one of the guests. It was an exciting day and one I will never forget. I took a beating on my overall score but did manage to par the famous "Church Pew" hole.

How golf has made me more self-aware: To be successful in golf, you're challenged to be very much in tune with what you are doing at all times. Just when you think instinct and repetitive insights should kick in and get you through, you lose concentration and duff one 10 feet to the left. Playing with others adds to the complexity. I would parallel this learning and adapting in golf with learning and adapting as a leader in business. You have to have patience when things don't go the way they should — reset and don't make the same mistake twice. You have to help others when they're lost — "I think your ball is behind that second elm tree over there." Learning in both golf and business for me at this stage of my career is centered around making adjustments as I go to fine-tune — not to be perfect, but to improve the outcome and my experience.

How golf has helped me develop business relationships: I was working on a large project, and I had trouble connecting with a doctor who was a subject matter expert on the team. We would have trouble understanding one another. He liked the long, thoughtful answer and I was a "get to the point" person. He was always in my area on business travel, spending most of his time on the road. We went out for a cocktail and that helped, we became better friends, but we didn't really fix the rhythm-of-work problem. One day I invited him to play a round of golf. We rented clubs for him and headed to the course. What do you think our game was like? Pretty much the same as it was in the office: I would walk up and swing the ball without practicing, not always with great success, but I would keep hitting anyway. He would take a few practice swings, contemplate the shot, and talk a lot in between the shots. He was calm, I was ready to go! It took a few holes and I can't say our level of play improved, but we found our balance. I relaxed and chatted more, and he and I had a very enjoyable time. That carried back to the office, and I made adjustments in my approach to working with him.

Advice for budding golfers: Don't wait to have a perfect swing. Get out and enjoy playing. Take the time first to learn the etiquette that is so important to the rhythm of the game — know the rules and study the experience. You don't have to shoot a low score to have an enjoyable round. Just play the game. I once received this advice: "You don't practice and play enough to get that mad at your game." I was playing with a coworker and friend, and I was becoming increasingly agitated that my iron shots were splaying all over the place and nothing was going right. When he said that to me, he added, "I go to the range and hit a hundred balls at least three times a week, and I play at least once a week, and I hit horrible shots all the time." Anger and frustration don't belong on the course. It's just a game, so relax and enjoy it.

15

GOLF ALTERNATIVES

Perhaps the industry needs to reconsider some of its criteria when it comes to measuring participation in golf. There should be a re-thinking of what having a golf experience means, and it shouldn't be defined by whether people play nine or 18 holes ... or even whether they visit a golf course.

Technology is so advanced today that we can turn our mobile phones into virtual experience devices. Some of the video games available on the market focus on a virtual golf experience, and their popularity ensure there will be more to come. While we certainly want people to go outside and play some "real" golf, the fact that they are participating in a golf experience should count.

Which brings us to the topic of this chapter, golf alternatives. There are all kinds of golf-related activities you can use to keep your golf relationships alive with clients other than playing a traditional round out on the course. Here are some ideas from Dave:

PROFESSIONAL GOLF TOURNAMENT

If you're lucky enough to live in an area that hosts a PGA or LPGA tour event, you can secure spectator passes to the tournament and take a client. I have the good fortune to live where there are three big events: the PGA Tour's Waste Management Phoenix Open, the LPGA JTBC Founders Cup, and the Champions Tour's Schwab Cup.

I take people to all of them. It's a great way to introduce a novice to the excitement of the game and to score points with your avid golfer associates by getting them up close and personal with players they usually see only on television. If you do your homework, you can figure out the best vantage points and even help your guests get a few autographs.

I have found the best days to go are the practice rounds or pro-am days. The atmosphere is usually more casual and it's easier to get around. I like to hang out at the practice tee. You can watch how the pros warm up, and you are most likely to see almost everyone who's playing. It might cost a bit more to secure the passes, but the impression it makes will more than pay off.

GOLF ENTERTAINMENT COMPLEXES

Another recent development on the golf scene is the combining of entertainment with a golf experience. The focus is on fun and social interaction, but the activity is golf. Well, at least there is a golf club and a ball involved.

Topgolf is sweeping the United States and the United Kingdom. The company's multi-story dining and entertainment venues boast "No experience required." Although there is a driving range of sorts involved, the game is quite different from traditional golf. Participants rent private "bays" by the hour where they can play a variety of fun games displayed on a big screen. Each location has a full bar and restaurant as well as meeting rooms and corporate memberships.

Dewey's Indoor Golf and Sport Grill is another concept that is taking off. This company provides a sports bar theme with a virtual golf component. Separate simulators allow individuals and groups to "play" famous courses such as Pebble Beach or the Old Course at St. Andrews. The simulators make for a pretty realistic experience, while the atmosphere provides a relaxed social environment perfect for chatting about business or simply getting to know someone better. And, unlike most golf courses, these venues are open well after the sun goes down.

CHARITY GOLF EVENTS

Playing in charity golf events is another great way to meet new people or to bring your own group to a golf experience that isn't just about the score. Most of the time these are played in a scramble format, which takes the pressure off people who are not as confident in their golf scores as others.

Inevitably, each player hits at least one of those great shots that nets the team a birdie or even an eagle.

These events are a great way to build positive public relations for you and your company. And there's the added benefit of donating to a cause.

You can find charity golf events by checking the activities listing in your local news outlets, or by asking people who are involved in charity work whether they know of any coming up. Golf equipment stores usually carry fliers for upcoming events as well.

BRING YOUR OWN PARTY

If you're looking for other ways to immerse your potential clients in a golf experience, be creative. Use the common denominator of golf as a starting point and then look for other non-traditional ways to express what you want to achieve. Organize a private golf class with six or more sessions that meet every week. Host a party to watch a tournament on TV that's too far away to attend. Go to a practice range together and make it competitive to keep it interesting and add some excitement. Have a business lunch at a golf course. Host a putting challenge at a miniature golf course.

Even if you don't get to hit a ball, being in the atmosphere can still add an element of relaxation. If you do belong to a private club, look for members-only activities where you can bring your prospects.

These are just a few examples of ways to enjoy a golf experience with colleagues or clients without spending the time or money required to play a round. You are only limited by your imagination. The more you're on the lookout for unique ways to connect through golf, you'll be surprised by what will emerge.

ON COURSE WITH ... SUE MCMURDY
EXECUTIVE ADVISOR, ENDEAVOR MANAGEMENT
CO-FOUNDER, BUSINESS GOLF ACADEMY

Why I play golf: Friends of my parents owned a golf course, and their daughter was my friend. At a very early age, when my family played golf, I played with Barbie dolls in the clubhouse with my friend. At about age eight, I put away the dolls and joined in on the game. I got to play with my father and compete with my two older brothers. As I began to play more, my aunt, an accomplished golfer, encouraged me to learn and play the game well if I was going to play at all. The better I played, the more fun it became and the more opportunities I had to make new friends, travel and play in junior tournaments and stand out. Not many girls played the game at that time, and I got noticed. I was also the first girl to play on a boys' golf team in the state of New York.

Golf is a game for a lifetime and THE game of my lifetime. I played golf with my family growing up and met my husband through the game. I play golf with my son, his wife and my grandsons. Golf was an amazing asset to me in my professional life. I played some competitive golf, met lifelong and famous friends through the game, and enjoy it now in my semi-retirement. I co-founded the Business Golf Academy with LPGA Player Missie Berteotti when I first retired to advance individuals in business golf, building confidence and competence. My relationship with the game varied as my life changed over the years. At times I have played more and practiced more, and at other times I was a once-a-week golfer. I spent a few years hating the game, but that is quite a small portion of a 50-year relationship. I doubt there is any other activity in which a person can play and compete for such a long duration.

> *The sense of accomplishment in a round well played or in achieving performance goals in business delivers great satisfaction.*
>
> — Sue McMurdy,
> Co-Founder,
> Business Golf Academy

How golf has helped me in business: I spent 35 years in financial services as CEO of a technology services company and executive vice president and chief information officer for a New York Stock Exchange-traded regional bank holding company. The fact that I played golf and was an accomplished player gained attention for my organization that gave us similar stature as organizations much larger in size. Golf levels the playing field in business relationship development, somewhat like the Internet does in the online marketplace. During rounds of golf, I have been part of initial conversations regarding bank acquisitions with chairmen and CEOs. I've discussed the changing of the entire geological landscape regarding shifting of tectonic plates with the president of exploration for an international oil company. And I've been able to broach some very difficult subjects with fellow executives.

How golf has made me more self-aware: We don't become good in our professional lives without discipline, hard work, good execution, strategic partnerships and an environment where we are able to perform without fear. The same formula works for golf. Successful business professionals who wish to be better at golf need to apply the same process improvement strategies with the sport as they do on the job. Great course architects design golf holes that present a variety of challenges requiring strategy and skill, and the same can be said for our businesses and our lives. The sense of accomplishment in a round well played or in achieving performance goals in business delivers great satisfaction.

How golf has helped me develop business relationships: Business is absolutely about building trusted relationships, and golf is the best relationship-building activity. I was a client of a very large software company. The chief technical strategy officer was someone I found very difficult to talk to. He was scary smart and not the best at carrying on a conversation. I discovered that he was interested in golf. At our next advisory board meeting, which always included golf, I asked to be put in the same group and ride on a cart together. During the four hours of the round of golf, we broke through our communications barrier. It became easier to speak about difficult technical issues, and we were able to associate them to some of our difficult golf situations.

Advice for novice golfers: Set realistic goals for golf, and the goal is not a score. The score is merely an outcome of the process of golf. Find someone at the same stage in the game as you are and learn together, play and practice together, encourage each other, and have fun together. Laugh at yourself!

Advice for making golf part of your business plan if you don't play the game: As a golfer, I would say you're missing out on a lot of fun. However, there may be instances where you just cannot play the game. Here are a few ideas.

First, it may be good to know that the game of golf generates more charitable contributions, by far, than all other sports combined. A win-win for you may be to get involved this way. You must learn the language of the game, understand how and where the game is played, who are the key players and sponsors, and how the business of golf operates. Reading about golf in books and magazines, researching golf on the Internet, watching the golf channel and listening to PGA Tour Radio are great ways to learn. I believe it is quite safe to say volunteers to help in charitable causes are very welcomed. Find a charity golf event in your area that aligns with your company or your personal mission, and connect with the leadership. They will certainly help you from there. Then put out invitations to the charity event to individuals with which you wish to develop a business relationship. You are there as a volunteer/leader, your group gets to see you doing great work for charity, and your associates get to play golf.

Another easy way is to buy tickets to a great golf event or buy a hospitality venue for entertaining. There is a wide price range to this type of option, but it can be very effective in the per-person cost to entertain for a day. You must think about how to get a "Yes" to your invitation to the golf event. Consider how avid a golfer or how interested in golf your potential client may be. Every person who knows anything about golf will say yes to an invitation to the U.S. Open Championship or The Masters Tournament. You will have to figure out the appropriate match for your target and the venue for your invitation.

My final suggestion involves a longer-term commitment but will create many opportunities for relationship-building and the opportunity to get involved in the game and help grow the sport. Golf associations rely on volunteers for their existence. They need marketing expertise, financiers, technical assistance and all management disciplines. Sign up as a volunteer. This option may not offer the invitation opportunities of the other suggestions, but many individuals compete in the events, and The National Golf Foundation tells us that eight in 10 individuals who play golf are business decision-makers. This will put you in close proximity to them.

Good luck!

16

THE LAST PUTT

As the final putt settles to the bottom of the cup on the 18th green, you might think, "Ahh, time to relax." You've played 18 holes of flawless business golf. You and your guests have had a great time. You played well (or not), and you can tell as you shake hands — removing your cap and sunglasses while looking them in the eye — that your guests genuinely enjoyed your company.

As you leave the green and head to the cart, you might feel like the pressure is off and you are, so to speak, off the clock. But you would be absolutely wrong.

There have been more bogeys made at the 19th hole than you might think. In fact, we look at what happens just after the last putt has dropped as the most important part of the day. Here is a description of what you want to experience:

> *I was playing with the chairman of my board and we were hosting a potential investor in the company. A few questions about the business surfaced throughout the round, but it was the 19th hole that made the difference.*
>
> *After having spent more than four hours on the course, we sat down at a table on the outside patio. We were away from the TVs inside, and now the questions became more focused. As we reminisced about the round, we began to talk about the future of the company and how he could be a part of it. The glow of the day had a halo effect on our conversation, and we were able to successfully propose that he join our venture.*

You need to finish strong to make this a successful business golf day. As you drive toward the clubhouse, stay focused. Make sure the outside service personnel or caddies are taken care of with an appropriate gratuity and that they ensure your guests' clubs are cleaned and ready to put into the trunk. Then you escort your guest into the 19th hole for a beverage and some time to reminisce about the day. Here are some tips from Dave about making the experience memorable:

A GIFT FOR YOUR GUESTS

This is the time I like to present my guest with a small gift — a reminder of the day we shared on the links. This can be anything from a logoed shirt or cap from your club or course to a divot tool with your company's name on it or logoed balls. Just make sure that what you present is top quality and something your guests will use or, better yet, show off to someone else.

The quality of the gift is a reflection of you, so quality matters. It should also be unique enough to remind someone of you.

ALCOHOLIC BEVERAGES

When it comes to drinking while playing business golf, I always keep in mind that I am working — not in the sense that it's a day at the office, but working nonetheless. I let my guests order first and take my cue from what they get. If it's a beer, I'll order a beer. If it's a glass of wine or something stronger, I'll order the same.

The key point here is that you need to be aware of staying in control. We've heard countless stories of 19th hole situations getting out of hand. In one instance, a guest got pulled over after a few too many drinks consumed while playing in a company-sponsored event. The DUI and subsequent dismissal from his job resulted in the company never doing business with the host again.

Now that is an extreme example, but there are plenty of other stories about situations that ended up negatively affecting the business relationship simply because the 19th hole got out of hand. Your goal is to create a lasting memory, not an incident.

One more thing: Make sure you pick up the tab and control consumption for you and your guest to be polite. While you're enjoying that drink and replaying the highlights of the day on the course, this is the time to work into the conversation the next steps.

BUSINESS CONVERSATION

Remember, there was an objective for calling this "meeting on the greens." I'm not suggesting that you pull out a contract to be signed or ask for the sale, but you do need to come to some agreement on the next steps.

You can accomplish this by making a statement like, "I really enjoyed playing with you today and getting to know a bit more about your company. Could we set up a time in the next week or so for me to come to your office and maybe brainstorm some opportunities to work together?" or "This was great being able to spend time with you on the course, and I look forward to doing it again in the near future. I would also like to schedule some time to talk about some opportunities between our companies. When would be a good time for us to meet?"

The follow-through isn't just important when it comes to your golf swing … it is everything when it comes to seizing the opportunity presented at the end of a business golf day. There aren't many other opportunities that I know of where you get to spend so much quality time with a prospective or valued client, and to not capitalize by defining next steps is a waste of your time and your company's dollars.

FUTURE PLANS

After you've settled the tab and bid your guest adieu, you can finally relax. You have finished your shift and can head home. The scratch handicap business golfer isn't quite finished, though.

I like to do a little debrief of the day while things are still fresh in my mind. I use a voice recording app on my phone to save interesting takeaways from the day that will help me formulate the key points for our next meeting. I also like to spend a little time reflecting on the day and what I might do differently in future rounds. I look at it as though I am reviewing my round: There are always a couple of shots I could have approached differently or executed better, just as there are certain situations I might have handled differently with my guest or things I could have done better to make the experience more enjoyable.

TROUBLESHOOTING TIPS

What we've described so far is how a typical business golf day plays out. But just like a day at the office, your perfectly planned golf day can fall victim to hijacking by outside influences.

Be prepared if your guest can't make it to the 19th hole — or worse, has to leave in the middle of the round. There are a lot of times when kids need to be picked up, a phone call from the office has your guest needing to make a sudden exit, or play has taken longer than expected. These factors can sabotage your best-laid plans.

So you need to be prepared to improvise depending on the situation. Walk your guests to the car and ask, "Can I call you tomorrow?" or offer a rain check for lunch since your guest didn't have time to grab something after the round. Do whatever you need to do to secure the next step. Be sure not to waste the opportunity simply because your guest had to cut the day short.

Another great way to keep the buzz going is to make sure you snap a few pictures on your smartphone that you can send to your guests the next day. This will help keep the conversation alive even if your guest needs to make a quick exit. Always use caution, though, when it comes to posting pictures on social media sites. Sometimes your guests may not have told their supervisors that the business meeting they were attending was on the golf course.

ON COURSE WITH ... TONY MARAMARCO
CFA MANAGING DIRECTOR, PORTFOLIO ADVISOR, NWQ

In the early 1980s, Jon Simonian was working as an institutional accounts salesman at Morgan Stanley and decided that two of his client-friends, Dave Salerno and I, needed to meet each other. Dave was running the Equity Management Group at MassMutual in Springfield, Mass., and had a position open for a stock analyst. I was chomping at the bit to advance in my career from Connecticut National Bank in Hartford.

Jon invited us to meet for a round of golf at the Farmington Country Club, where he then played matchmaker very successfully. Dave eventually hired me — despite, or maybe because of, my taking money from him and Jon that day — and that round of golf launched my 21-year career at MassMutual.

When I managed money professionally, I was continually aware of the risk/reward presented by every holding in my clients' portfolios, much the same as I try to be aware of the risk/reward of every shot in a round of golf, although sometimes emotions get in the way. I am conservative by nature, and my clients expected and appreciated such an approach from me as their money manager. They did not expect to see any snowmen on their investment reports.

> *Don't screw this up. Make three well-placed shots to get to the green, two-putt, get out of Dodge, never regret having attempted anything more dramatic or risky, and watch the Masters for the rest of your life in peace.*
>
> — Tony Maramarco,
> CFA Managing Director,
> Portfolio Advisor, NWQ

So it was no surprise when I said to myself, standing on the 13th tee at Augusta National on Election Day 1992: "Don't screw this up. Make three well-placed shots to get to the green, two-putt, get out of Dodge, never regret having attempted anything more dramatic or risky, and watch the Masters for the rest of your life in peace."

For my clients, I played conservatively, hitting for singles and doubles (pars) and the occasional triple (birdie) or home run (eagle). It's not a particularly exciting approach, but my clients were happy and I was happy as well — and maintained a single-digit handicap.

P.S. — I parred the 13th hole that day ... and if I ever get back to Augusta National, I'll play it the same way.

17

THE 19TH HOLE

You have one goal and one goal only when you hit the 19th hole, and that is to secure your next step with your colleague, client or prospect. There are so many things that could derail this step that you have to be conscious of how the opportunity could get away from you. An ill-timed trip to the restroom could result in you seeing the taillights of your guest's car headed out of the parking lot before you know it.

The 19th hole, for those of you who don't know, is the stop at the bar or lounge where you revisit the highs and lows of the round and report on the final score for each player or team. If you were playing a serious round of golf, it's also the time you settle up on who owes how much to whom. And, unlike with other competitive events, the winner buys the drinks. So don't gloat too much about your low score.

If you really want to manage the time to maximize what you want out of it, prepare in advance. Make a stop at the bar before you even tee off, and see if you can reserve a table ahead of time. See if you can get one in a quieter part of the lounge where the conversation is not overwhelmed by TVs, video games, live music or other events that might be happening at the club. Pre-pay for a round of drinks so it's harder for your guests to turn down the invitation to join you when the round is over — and that also can ensure better service, especially if the tip is paid in advance.

One thing to be sensitive to is whether or not your guests drink alcohol. You might have already picked up on this while out on the course, but make sure you don't make the person uncomfortable by insisting he or she have some alcohol. In fact, make it easy by including a non-alcoholic beverage choice when you ask, "What can I get you? A beer, wine, mixed drink, iced tea, diet cola?" That will take the pressure off of someone who doesn't want to be the odd person out by not indulging.

This should be a social time, not a time to over-serve yourself, so watch how much you drink, too. That will be a signal to others about your ability to handle choices and manage your own behavior. There's nothing worse than a drunken host.

Make sure as you're gathering that you get the right seat so you can have a side conversation with your guest. While everyone is gathering, you could end in the worst seat because you've been organizing the gathering with the bar staff and not watching while everyone else grabs the prime seats. So this positioning should be the first thing on your mind as you arrive. Say to your prospect, "Let's sit here. Let's throw our hats on these chairs so we claim them."

You don't need much from the 19th hole, but you do want to get agreement on the next step. Be prepared for what choices you want to propose, and don't leave it up to the other person to figure it out. Be in charge and say things like, "I'm so glad you were able to play today. It was really a lot of fun having you in our foursome. I do have a few things I'd like to talk to you about. What does your calendar look like in the next couple of weeks, and maybe we could grab a cup of coffee and I'll fill you in on what I'd like to discuss."

Have your business card handy and give it to him or her, which subconsciously reinforces that this was a business event.

Now, you're going to have to learn how to dance based on the situation, but keep in mind the goal is to establish a next step. To get to this, your guest needs to feel good about the round he or she just played, so find ways to compliment something … anything. Guests need to hear, even if they don't really believe it, something that will take the sting out of a bad performance. Give them a plausible excuse, such as, "You played really well for someone who doesn't get to play very often. I was impressed!" At least you're being polite. If others you were playing with go overboard in the ribbing and banter, help protect the other person's ego by not piling on.

On occasion, you may be able to have that business conversation right then and there, but keep in mind these variables as to whether or not you take advantage of that moment:

- **Is your guest on a tight time schedule?** If so, then you're adding pressure by insisting that he or she join you at the 19th hole. Ask, "Do you have time to join me, or should we schedule another time in the near future?" You'll actually gain points here with your sensitivity to his or her other priorities.

- **Who else is at the 19th hole?** It may be difficult to have a business conversation if there is the potential for a competitor or even another colleague from the same firm overhearing your discussion. You could say, "Should we step outside where it's a little more private to discuss this?" Just keep in mind that your guest may want to have the conversation but feels restricted by the open environment.

- **The noise level may be a barrier.** If your guest has a hearing issue, then he or she may be nodding but is really missing every other word. Your guest may also find the noise level simply annoying. If you're more than 20 years younger than the other person, you might miss this issue.

- **Control the agenda**. If you have been attending an event sponsored by someone else, then you are hostage to the agenda of the host for the event. If this is the case, strike early with your question about a next step. Otherwise the event organizers' game plan will close out your opportunity to gain any value out of the 19th hole, and before you know it, your guest will beg off and head home. If this is the case and you need to stay, walk your guest to his or her car. That will give you a few moments to get to your next step.

- **Look for opportunities.** When you are at a professional tournament, it's sometimes like you're at the 19th hole the entire day. But it's amazing how business fades into the background and the excitement of the event takes over. This is to be expected, so work with it. You really want to have your conversation as early as possible and before any distractions, such as massive quantities of adult beverages, make it impossible to get the person's focus. Try to get the guest away from the activity so you can get a few minutes of his or her attention. Have a plan where you can go get some food, visit the booths or walk to a different part of the course even if you're in the stands. Your goal is to get undivided attention so you secure your next step. It may only take two minutes or it may take the better part of an afternoon.

There are also four different approaches you want to keep in mind. Some people just want you to be clear and direct about what you're asking, and they'll respond in kind. Others are much more thoughtful and will never make a commitment in the moment. With them, you need to plant a seed and then give it time to germinate.

Some prospects want to know all the details associated with what you're asking. If it's something simple like, "Let's meet for lunch," they want to know the date, time and place as well as the purpose for the lunch, so you need to be very specific. There are others who are easy to get to a next step if they perceive it as fun and sociable. Make sure that your "ask" is couched in statements that feel upbeat, positive and something it would be hard to say no to because the fun factor is high.

Business golf is all about building relationships so you can work with them. Relationships based on mutual trust and respect take time. However, spending a day on a course or at a tournament will accelerate the ability to get to this strong relationship with your prospect, client, potential partner, vendor, supplier or key colleague.

For you, this is not a recreational activity. Because golf simulates what happens in the business world, you have just spent a day at work. Your character, sociability, trustworthiness and leadership potential were all scrutinized while you were on the course. Don't blow it at the 19th hole. Instead, use this opportunity as the way to move your business forward by getting agreement on the next step.

ON COURSE WITH ... WILL GRANNIS
MANAGING DIRECTOR, CLOUD CTO OFFICE, GOOGLE

Why I play golf: I play golf for three reasons: first, because all my friends were playing after college and they wanted to make fun of someone; second, because I love getting outside and consciously setting aside four to five hours to enjoy some of the most beautiful scenery in any town; third, because it's as much a mental challenge as a physical one.

How golf has helped me in business: The first (real) job interview I ever had (not counting pizza delivery) was on a golf course. I was leaving the military and had no idea what I was going to do with my life. A friend of my father-in-law was interested in chatting with me about a potential role in his company. (Un)fortunately, he wanted to have the interview on a golf course — and not just any course, but the Stadium Course at TPC Scottsdale. As if playing golf wasn't enough to fray my nerves a bit, meeting someone for the first time, on a golf course, with a job on the line, and having a small and growing family that was counting on me for said job ... well, it wasn't what I would call "something I looked forward to." But the day came and went, and my soon-to-be boss and I had a great time smoking cigars and telling stories (lies). The connection we made on the course carried over to the 19th hole, where he wrote an offer on the back of a business card and that was that. Now, part of me thinks he was so impressed by my miracle two-shots-to-reach-the-island-green that he had to hire me. But looking back, it is clear that it was the moments where we shared stories, laughed a bit, and he saw how I dealt with pressure, nerves, anxiety and some less-than-awesome (terrible, really) shot-making that probably made the difference. As I've aged a bit,

> *One unexpected discovery is that golf also reminds me to be comfortable in my own skin, to not try too hard to emulate someone else's swing.*
>
> — Will Grannis, Managing Director, Cloud CTO Office, Google

122

I notice how much those things matter, and a golf course is a fabulous window into someone's character.

How golf has made me more self-aware: I am now very comfortable cursing in public. Really, though, golf has taught me about patience, planning, and how thousands of swings are required to build in the memory it takes to hit big shots under pressure. The same is true in life ... it takes a lot of paddling underneath the surface to keep things placid on top. Just because we don't always see the work it requires, that doesn't mean it isn't required. One unexpected discovery is that golf also reminds me to be comfortable in my own skin, to not try too hard to emulate someone else's swing. And my best results come from days where I feel like I'm playing my game, in control, with a strategy. Same at work. My best days are when I have a plan, execute the plan as best I can, and then just look to keep improving.

Advice for novices: Don't start playing golf if you don't like to drink, because it will start both habits concurrently. Honestly, it reminds me a of a concept I learned at business school some years ago, about integrating the different circles of your life, and how finding ways to integrate them can lead to really amazing results (by Stewart Friedman, who wrote *Total Leadership*). Find an opportunity to get golf into your life, and then look for ways to integrate it into your personal and professional life. My love of golf has strengthened my relationship with my wife and youngest daughter, led to some very close business mentors, and allowed me to walk miles along some of the most beautiful places on earth.

18

THE FOLLOW-THROUGH

We've come to the end of our round, and hopefully you have gained some new ideas, both strategic and tactical, that will help you get *Back On Course* and realize a significant business return on the investment you've made in the game. As you approach the 18th hole, it's not unusual to feel fatigued and then begin to find yourself slipping backward in your performance. The same is true in business. We often give up in the final stages just because we're worn out. The main thought that applies to both business and golf is: Finish strong!

If you played your 19th hole well, you should already have your next steps under way with your client or prospect. Make sure you follow through, because you have the opportunity to reinforce your credibility by doing exactly what you said you were going to do. If you promised a picture, find the time to drop by your guest's office to drop it off. If you said you'd provide an introduction to someone important to your guest, make sure you do it. There is nothing that will get a business relationship off track faster than failure to follow through. And because so many people promise but never deliver, you will build loyalty when your deeds match your words.

Use your love of the game to continue to build the relationship with your business colleague. Forward emails of anecdotes, pictures, cartoons or short stories that have nothing to do with business but show that you really do value the relationship. The more you can give your potential clients a reason to smile, the more ingrained in their memory you become.

INVITE YOUR GUESTS TO RECONNECT

One way to take the relationship to another level is to ask the client to join you in supporting a charity event. Get involved together on a board or a task team that gives you a shared experience. Giving back is always rewarding on lots of levels, making it a great way to build a stronger bond. Or keep it simple and just ask your prospect to join you for a charity event. It may be harder to say no to something that has a higher value than a simple round of golf.

We've focused a lot on using golf as a way to build relationships, but at some point you have to turn this into business value. You've invested your time and the company's money, and now it's time to make it worthwhile.

While the golf course or club may not be the best place to discuss the deal, it is still important to tee up that conversation. The most important part of the process is to know what you want and then craft a statement that asks for the meeting with clarity about its purpose. For example, you might say, "Steve, I would really like to find some time to talk with you about a business opportunity that could benefit both of us. What would work for your calendar?" Or this one: "Carol, I know you're looking for a solution to your data management challenges, and I have some ideas I know would interest you. I'll give your office a call on Monday to set up a time to show you what I'm thinking would work for you." Here's another: "I know you already have a financial advisor, but I'd like to get a few minutes of your time to show you some unique money management techniques that most other agents overlook. I'm sure I could add value to your desire to ensure that your financial resources are properly managed."

CLOSE THE DEAL

In keeping with the iMapGolf model discussed in *Chapter 3: Power Tools for Success*, there are four different ways to close the deal. If you stick to your tried and true, you may be missing opportunities because someone is reacting to you and not to the deal you're offering. The math symbols you learned in grade school provide a simple way to remember these four different approaches. You should have picked up on all of these while you played golf with your prospect.

The first is the **plus sign.** For some people you need to add up all of the intangible benefits they will receive through your proposal, and then you need to ask, yes or no? They also like long lists, so make sure you don't miss anything tangible that they will get with the deal you're proposing. You'll know to use this approach if the person you're trying to influence is impatient and just wants to get to the bottom line. You will have seen this need for speed on the golf course, so get to the bottom line fast.

The second is the **minus sign.** These are people who don't want to lose, so create a scenario where they may miss out on something if they don't make a decision right away. They respond well to urgency, so they appreciate "Order by midnight tonight" kinds of offers. Throw in added benefits that will go away if they don't do the deal now. You will know these people from the golf course as the risk takers. They love a bet and will take chances on shots they've never succeeded with before.

The third is the **division sign.** People with this characteristic are into data, metrics, details and processes. You have to present your proposed deal with a lot of minutia spelled out from every angle possible. And you dare not be wrong with any of your details, because these people don't miss a thing. Thorough preparation is essential for your proposed business deal with this person — and put it in writing so you can easily review the data. When you play golf with people like this, you'll notice they take their time to evaluate information like wind direction, yardage and which club to play. They also know the rules and make sure you all play by them.

The fourth is the **multiplication sign.** These are the toughest people to close a deal with because they are always thinking of new ideas. They find it difficult to make decisions because the variables are unending. The relationship you have with these people will make a difference in whether or not you close your deal because they do business with people they trust. If you're in that close circle of trusted advisors, you're golden. But it's tough to get there. It takes a lot of time listening and asking questions, which will demonstrate you care more about them than any deal. You will have seen their behavior on the golf course as somewhat reserved in their interactions with others and concerned about how others were judging their performance.

You can probably identify one of these four styles as your natural approach to doing a business deal. To be effective with a broader range of people, you need to learn to recognize what all of the types respond to best and then adapt your style to match what works for them. This will ensure all of your deals close!

SHOW ROI FOR YOUR ORGANIZATION

The last and most important part of the follow-up is to make sure you show your ROI to those in your corporate entity who keep track of money spent vs. money earned. They often dwell in the accounting or finance departments, and it's not unusual for them to place little value on the game of golf. That's because no one has run the numbers for them. To really get business *Back On Couse,* we have to provide conclusive evidence that an investment pays off. You must sell this internally.

Being able to sell internally requires that you start keeping track of what's happened. In your reports, or however you track your business development activities, be able to show how that lead progressed through the sales funnel, and link any and all golf activities that helped move it through. When you have a sale, partnership or business opportunity close, don't forget to credit golf for being one of the tools you used to make this happen. If you can find a way to demonstrate this in formal reports, great! But at a minimum, include the reference in your conversations and presentations so you give proper credit to the game.

For example, let's say you took some prospects to the Phoenix Open. Show how much it cost per person for the outing. Then start tracking phone calls, visits, demos, proposals that never would have occurred if you hadn't hosted them at the event. This type of data can help a company see the value in sponsorship of an event or even just paying your expense account.

Here's an example from Connie:

I started SSI 25 years ago as a small, boutique consulting firm. When I stumbled on the value of golf for building our client base, we started hosting Executive Golf Schools as our marketing event. We held them at high-end resorts and invited local executives to come spend a day with us.

We had a scripted process, which started with a list and then a cold call to find out whether that senior leader was a golfer. This was not an inexpensive marketing campaign. However, we closed 78 percent of the attendees we followed up with after the event. These were corporations that were household names and were usually out of reach for a small, boutique consulting firm.

In business, just as with your golf swing, your follow-through is key. It's your way to finish strong!

ON COURSE WITH ... RANDALL REED
PRESIDENT AND CEO, REED ENTERPRISES

How I began playing golf: I got started in golf to do business. I became a Ford dealer when I was 29 years old in Dallas, Texas, and golf was a great way to get involved. Ford would put on events, and they had a program called Executive Golf Outing. I had swung a few clubs as a kid, but I'd never really played 18 holes until I got into the Ford program. You look at the 10-year-old-kids now, and they square their shoulders and set their hips and follow through on their swings. That was not me. I was all arms. I was a wreck. But I realized what a great opportunity golf would give me to network and connect. I bought clubs and kept playing even though I was horrible. I shot a 125 to 130. I found out later that this is kind of average for someone who has never played. So I was average. But I loved it. Once you get the bug, you want to get better.

Why I play golf: I have partners who go to those events now. Today I play for relaxation and fun. I own 16 businesses, so golf gives me a way to unwind from work. For those four hours on the course, you totally disengage from your thoughts, your concerns and your problems. On the ninth hole, you remember, "Oh yeah, I have this issue. Oh well."

> " But I realized what a great opportunity golf would give me to network and connect.
>
> — Randall Reed,
> President and CEO,
> Reed Enterprises

How golf has helped me develop relationships: My wife was a tennis player, and I got her interested in golf. Now she's a phenomenal golfer and wants to play more than I do. We've taken lessons and have gone to the best golf schools in the country. We split our time now between Colorado and Arizona, and at our place in Sedona we can play 50 to 75 rounds in five months. We started an event called the Vortex Open, where we play a scramble. We bring together 30 to 45 friends and it keeps growing. You'll see people in their 40s who have never swung a club in their lives, and a lot of them go back and start playing golf. I think of it as a brotherhood and a community — a tight community.

How golf has made me more self-aware: I went through Dave and Connie's iMapGolf seminar and gained good insight. I'm a perfectionist, and unless I'm doing it exactly right, I get frustrated. I'm the most enthusiastic person, so when I get to the course I'm all excited. I play a couple of good holes, but then I hit a bad shot and I dwell on it — and I do that in business, too. They've given me a key word to use when I get into that situation: B2B. It means "back to basics." Focus on the basics and you'll get back into your groove. It's almost like a reset. That helps a lot.

Advice for novice golfers: Once you get in, it's addicting. You will get addicted. Here's my advice: Make sure you devote plenty of time to the sport and take plenty of lessons. Get the right equipment, and that includes the right attire. If you dress the part, you'll be amazed at how much easier it is to perform. You really only have to look good on holes one and 18 anyway. Practice before you go out on the course. Don't just jump out on the first tee without warming up. It takes me three or four holes to settle down if I do that. Don't practice all day on your driver. That's such a nominal part of your game. Instead, 60 yards from the hole is where the action is. Practice your short game. That's what I've worked on the most this year. And just keep at it. Chances are you're one swing away from where you're supposed to be.

ABOUT THE AUTHORS

CONNIE CHARLES is the Founder and CEO of Strategic Solutions International, based in Newark, Delaware. She has been building successful corporate teams for Fortune 100 companies for 20 years and has put that expertise to use in an online portal called iMapMyTeam that permits companies to access the know-how and tools that ensure successful team selection and management. A companion portal, iMapGolf, puts the same science to work to show individuals how to improve their performance on the golf course for business or pleasure.

DAVE BISBEE is the General Manager and Director of Golf at Seven Canyons Golf Club in Sedona, Arizona, and a collaborator on iMapGolf. He is renowned for his ability to assess results relative to goals, facilitate changes that lead to success and help people develop personal competencies. He has worked with Fortune 1000 companies including Hewlett Packard, Merrill Lynch and IBM to motivate teams to respond successfully in an ever-changing business environment. He shows clients how the principles of playing better golf are the same that produce better business results.

If you're interested in working with Connie and Dave to get your business *Back On Course*, contact them at 1-800-815-0185 or send them an email at *info@iMapGolf.com.*

Here are some golf programs they lead:

DRIVE IT THROUGH THE GRASS CEILING

This program is designed specifically for executive women who recognize that the shortest road to the top may be the cart path. This event fast-tracks the learning experience by combining an easy-to-master approach to golf skills with the fundamentals of business etiquette for the golf course.

BUSINESS GOLF ESSENTIALS

You only have one shot at a first impression, and it's usually the first tee. Everyone hears about the deals made on the golf course. No one is talking about the business that was lost. This course teaches businesspeople how to put together an effective strategy for managing a round of golf that has a higher purpose than a low score.

THE TEAM TEE-OFF

Build a solid team in one day! If you believe the quality of relationships affects the performance of your group, the Team Tee Off is your perfect solution. Using the golf course as the classroom, participants learn how to work together in a competitive business simulation that tests their ability to deliver ROI. Golfers and non-golfers become equal partners in the exercise, which includes access to *iMapMyTeam*, a dashboard on interpersonal relationships.

NOTES

NOTES

Made in the USA
Middletown, DE
18 February 2019